D0638041

GAMBIT OPENING REPERTOIRE FOR WHITE

ABOUT THE AUTHOR

Eric Schiller, widely considered one of the world's foremost chess analysts, writers and teachers, is internationally recognized for his definitive works on openings. He is the author of more than 75 chess books including definitive studies of many chess openings and more than two dozen USCF (United States Chess Federation) best-sellers.

His major works include the prestigious *Batsford Chess Openings* with World Champion Garry Kasparov and Grandmaster Raymond Keene, and Cardoza Publishing's definitive series on openings, *World Champion Openings*, *Standard Chess Openings*, and *Unorthodox Chess Openings* — an exhaustive and complete opening library of more than 1700 pages! He's also the author of *Gambit Opening Repertoire for White, Gambit Opening Repertoire for Black*, and multiple other chess titles for Cardoza Publishing. (For updated listings of all chess titles published by Cardoza Publishing, go online to www.cardozapub.com, or for a complete listing of the author's books, to Eric Schiller's web site: www.chessworks.com)

Eric Schiller is a National and Life Master, an International Arbiter of F.I.D.E., winner of three state titles (California, Illinois, and Hawaii), and the official trainer for many of America's top young players. In 1996, he coached America's best players under 18 at the Chess World Championships. He has also presided over world championship matches, and runs prestigious international tournaments. His games have been featured in leading media including the venerable New York Times.

GAMBIT OPENING REPERTOIRE FOR WHITE

Eric Schiller

Cardoza Publishing

To all those who play chess for fun, for sport and for art!

Copyright © 1998 by Eric Schiller
- All Rights Reserved -

First Edition

Library of Congress Catalogue Card No: 97-67063
ISBN: 0-940685-78-7

CARDOZA PUBLISHING
PO Box 1500 Cooper Station, New York, NY 10276
Phone (718)743-5229 • Fax(718)743-8284 •
Email:cardozapub@aol.com
Web Site - www.cardozapub.com

Write for your free catalogue of gaming and chess books,
equipment, software and computer games.

TABLE OF CONTENTS

1. INTRODUCTION   **9**

2. THE WHITE GAMBIT   **10**

3. OVERVIEW   **12**

Gambits Against Black Replies   13
    Black Replies 1...e5   13
    Black Replies 1...e6   14
    Black Replies 1...c5   15
    Black Replies 1...c6   16
    Black Replies 1...d6   17
    Black Replies 1...Nf6   19
    Black Replies 1...Nc6   19
    Black Replies 1...d5   20
    Black Replies 1...b6   21

4. GÖRING GAMBIT – INTRODUCTION   **22**

Overview   22
Options at move 4   *24*
    Option 1: 4...Bc5   24
    Option 2: 4...Qe7   25
    Option 3: 4...Nge7   26
    Option 4: 4...d3   27
Options at move 5   *30*
    Option 1: 5...Nd5!?   30
    Option 2: 5...Ng8   31
    Option 3: 5...Ng4   32
    Option 4: 5...Qe7   33

5. GÖRING GAMBIT – ACCEPTED (PART ONE)   **38**

Overview   38
Options at move 5   *39*
    Option 1: 5...Bc5   39
    Option 2: 5...Nf6   40

6. GÖRING GAMBIT ACCEPTED (PART TWO)   42

Overview   42
Options at move 6   *43*
   Option 1: 6...Be6   43
   Option 2: 6...Be7   45
   Option 3: 6...Nf6   52

7. GÖRING GAMBIT ACCEPTED (PART THREE)   57

Overview   57
Options at move 6   *58*
   Option 1: 6...Qf6   58
   Option 2: 6...Bxc3+   59
   Option 3: 6...Nge7   60
   Option 4: 6...Nf6   61
Options at move 8   *65*
   Option 1: 8...Bg4   65
   Option 2: 8...Be6   67
   Option 3: 8...Qe7?   71
Options at move 13   *76*
   Option 1: 13...Nd7?   76
   Option 2: 13...Kh8   77
   Option 3: 13...Bd7   80

8. GÖRING GAMBIT DECLINED   83

Overview   83
Options at move 6   *84*
   Option 1: 6...Nf6   84
   Option 2: 6...Bg4   86

9. SICILIAN DEFENSE – HALASZ GAMBIT   93

Overview   93
Option at move 3   *94*
   Option: 3...d6   94
Options at move 4   *98*
   Option 1: 4...g6   98
   Option 2: 4...d5   99

10. FRENCH DEFENSE – ALAPIN GAMBIT   104

Overview   104

11. CARO-KANN DEFENSE – ULYSSES GAMBIT   109

Overview   109

Options at move 6   *111*
   Option 1: 6...Be7   111
   Option 2: 6...b5!?   112
   Option 3: 6...Nbd7   113

12. PIRC DEFENSE - SHORT ATTACK (PART ONE) **117**

Overview   117
Options at move 9   *119*
   Option 1: 9...c6   119
   Option 2: 9...Bf5   121
   Option 3: 9...c5   122
   Option 4: 9...e5   122
Options at move 11   *123*
   Option 1: 11...e6   124
   Option 2: 11...c6   124
   Option 3: 11...e5   125
   Option 4: 11...Bf5   126

13. PIRC DEFENSE - SHORT ATTACK (PART TWO) **129**

Overview   129
Options at move 7   *130*
   Option 1: 7...d5.   130
   Option 2: 7...f5.   131

14. PIRC DEFENSE - SHORT ATTACK (PART THREE) **135**

Overview   135
Options at move 6   *136*
   Option 1: 6...Nh5   136
   Option 2: 6...dxe5   137

15. MODERN DEFENSE – FOGUELMAN ATTACK **141**

Overview   141
Options at move 4   *142*
   Option 1: 4...c6   142
   Option 2: 4...Nd7   143
   Option 3: 4...e6   144
   Option 4: 4...c5!?   145

16. CZECH DEFENSE **148**

Overview   148
Options at move 4   *149*
   Option 1: 4...Bg4   149

Option 2: 4...Qc7   150
Option 3: 4...Nbd7   151
Option 4: 4...e6   152
Option 5: 4...d5   152
Option 6: 4...Qb6   153
Option 7: 4...e5   154
Option 8: 4...g6   155
Option at move 5   *157*
Option: 5...Nd5   157
Options at move 6   *159*
Option 1: 6...f5   159
Option 2: 6...Bf5   159
Options at move 7   *161*
Option 1: 7...e6   161
Option 2: 7...d5   162
Option 3: 7...g6   163
Option 4: 7...g5   163
Option 5: 7...Qd5   164
Option 6: 7...c5!?   164
Option 7: 7...dxe5   165

17. ALEKHINE DEFENSE – KREJCIK VARIATION   168
Overview   168

**18. SCANDINAVIAN DEFENSE –
TENNISON GAMBIT   171**
Overview   171
Options at move 3   *172*
Option 1: 3...e5   172
Option 2: 3...f5!?   173
Option 3: 3...Qd5   174
Option 4: 3...Bf5   177
Option 5: 3...Nf6.   177

19. OWEN DEFENSE   179
Overview   179

20. LAST THOUGHTS   183

SUGGESTIONS FOR FURTHER READING   184

INTRODUCTION

If you enjoy attacking from the very first move, you will be rewarded here with a powerful repertoire of brilliant gambits. I'm going to show you how to give up a bit of material, usually a single pawn, and in return, throw immediate attacking pressure on your opponent. Your sacrifice will bring you rapid development, control of the center, and open lines to use for your attack. This is pressure chess–one small mistake by Black and we'll crush his forces!

Gambits are the most exciting of the chess openings, and in this book, you'll learn how to effectively use such sharp weapons as the Göring Gambit (Accepted and Declined), Halasz Gambit, Alapin Gambit, Ulysses Gambit, Short Attack, and more, to use against the most popular defenses including the Sicilian, French, Scandinavian, Caro-Kann, Pirc, Alekhine, and a host of opening situations.

If you want to win at chess, you have to take some risks, and in the opening, gambits are a sure way to seize the initiative from the very start. You exchange a little material for some intangible but very powerful weapons, and increase the pressure until your opponent cracks.

The ideas and key concepts are clearly explained for each gambit, and I have provided example diagrams to illustrate each of the key positions. Even if you don't remember all of the analysis, you'll see the patterns at work, and at the chessboard, you'll be able to attack, attack, attack! Most of your opposition, unless they are experienced Masters, will find their defensive barriers falling quickly. Even the best players can be ambushed with these sharp openings. You can learn the entire repertoire at once, or use the various strategies individually, mixing and matching them with your current openings.

I have selected some fairly obscure ideas so that your gambits will have the added potency of a surprise attack. Not only will you find a carefully researched set of variations, I'll also share with you some secret ideas which have not been published anywhere else.

Using the tips in this book you'll not only get good results, but you'll enjoy every game as White as you smash opponent after opponent, often catching them completely unaware. You'll become a true gambiteer, well versed in the art of attack.

So read on, enjoy, and win!

THE WHITE GAMBIT

You will find an exciting selection of gambits for use by White in this book. These openings are not usually seen in Grandmaster competition, not because they are unsound, but because professional players rely on more effective means of fighting for an advantage in the opening, trading excitement for practical results. Most tournament players have used gambits as White at some time, and many club players have relied on them exclusively.

Generally, the privilege of offering a gambit belongs to White, who has the advantage of the first move. This means that we can more easily afford the luxury of giving up a pawn, because the momentum gained by the sacrifice is helped along by the right to move first. Giving up some material for space, tempo, or other intangible advantages is known as "compensation" and the merit of a gambit is determined by how much compensation is received for the material.

Sacrificing material for compensation is the trade-off a gambiteer makes in every game. Our opponents suffer tremendous pressure, even when they have an extra pawn or two. Usually, especially if they are amateurs, they will crack. Even professional players and famous theoreticians sometimes stumble when confronted with a gambit. Computers, unable to feel the heat, calmly calculate and usually can get through the opening unscathed. Sometimes, however, the long-term complications elude them. They tend not to appreciate positional compensation, such as forcing their king to f8 and locking in the rook at h8.

Most of the gambits you will meet here are objectively about equal. Neither White nor Black can claim a meaningful advantage, and each has chances for victory. In some cases we find ourselves with a slight disadvantage if Black manages to play all the right moves. These gambits are very sharp, and the position can turn to our advantage at the slightest slip on the part of our opponents.

The term "gambit" has been used for chess since the 16th century, when Ruy Lopez, best known for the ultra–orthodox Spanish Game. It comes from the Italian word *gambetto* which was used for a tricky maneuver in wrestling, basically tripping the opponent. It has entered our mainstream language with a meaning of a devious move used to open a game. Actually, there is nothing subtle about a gambit—it is a straightforward attempt to smash the enemy position.

Gambits may be accepted or declined. In accepting a gambit, the defender is prepared for a long defensive struggle, after which the extra material may be exploited in an endgame. Declining a gambit is safer, but it is usually the case that a positional price is paid and the opponent will get a promising position anyway.

The 19th century was filled with gambit play, which was part of the repertoire of most of the great players of the time, including Anderssen and Morphy. This was not simply a result of aggressive intentions on the part of the players, but because defensive technique was weak or non-existent. Because defenders had a hard time coping with threats, fans of gambits ("gambiteers") were able to score many victories. This led to a high reputation for gambit openings such as the King's Gambit (1.e4 e5; 2.f4.) and Evans Gambit (1.e4 e5; 2.Nf3 Nc6 ; 3.Bc4 Bc5; 4.b4).

One factor which played a major role was the social obligation to accept gambits. Declining was considered a dishonorable act of cowardice. Modern thinking attaches no stigma to declining a gambit. Indeed, many gambits should be declined because it is too dangerous to accept them, or declining leads to such a good position that it is the superior play. As White, we must not fall into the psychological trap of expecting our opponent to fall in with our gambit plans.

Although gambits play only a minor role in the professional ranks, for most chessplayers they remain the most popular of openings. They are fun to play and even a novice can sometimes produce an impressive attack or combination by using them. The enduring appeal of the gambit openings has not diminished in the age of the computer, either. Machines have a difficult time correctly evaluating compensation, and often underestimate a gambit..

Try out the openings you learn here in your games and keep pounding away at the enemy position. The battles will be bloody and draws will be rare. Play your games with a concentration on the weaknesses in the enemy position. Don't worry about regaining your material too quickly, but at the same time don't avoid positions where you recapture your investment while maintaining a superior position. Keep some open files for your rooks, point your bishops and knights in the right direction, and make sure your king is safe and your queen can join the fight quickly. You may well find that the enemy king falls into your hands before the opening is over!

OVERVIEW

We will open with the advance of the e-pawn to allow our pieces to develop quickly. Our knights can jump to c3 and f3, the bishop can come to c4 or b5, and the queen can operate from f3, g4, or h5. In particular, we want to get the light squared bishop involved in an attack on f7, since that is the most vulnerable spot in Black's formation. Additionally, e4 allows us to control the important d5 square.

TWENTY LEGAL BLACK RESPONSES TO 1.E4

1...e5 is the classical Double King Pawn opening.

1...c5 is the fighting Sicilian Defense, now the most popular move.

1...e6 is the solid French Defense, which can also turn very sharp quickly.

1...c6 is the quiet Caro-Kann Defense, which usually features endgame play.

1...d5, the Scandinavian Defense has been surging in popularity.

1...d6 is a flexible move which is often used in conjunction with a kingside fianchetto in the Czech Defense.

1...g6 is the hypermodern Lizard (or Modern Defense) where Black aims a bishop at the center.

1...Nc6 is the Nimzowitsch Defense, though Black has a variety of plans that can be used after 2.d4.

1...Nf6 is the once radical Alekhine, now pale by comparison with today's unorthodox variations.

1...b6 is the never fashionable Owen Defense. White can occupy the center without difficulty.

1...a6 is a flexible move which does not disclose Black's plans. It often leads by transposition to other openings.

1...Na6 is starting off in the wrong direction. The knight needs to be closer to the center.

1...a5 is simply irrelevant, in most cases. It contributes nothing to Black's game.

1...h6 is not a major structural liability, but it is a waste of time which gives White a chance to grab the center and develop quickly.

1...h5 is a premature weakening of the kingside. White can use the pawn for target practice.

1...Nh6 is a drunken knight move. The Black knight almost never belongs at h6, and after 2.d4 White threatens to capture it.

1...g5 is the Borg Defense, and though aggressive, it weakens Black's kingside.

1...f6 is an ugly move and it takes away the useful f6 square which is usually reserved for a knight.

1...b5 is a terrible move, giving up a pawn for nothing.

1...f5 is a move which loses a pawn and weakens the kingside at one blow. It is the worst reply to 1.e4.

Black has twenty legal responses, shown on the previous page, but only a few are respectable. The list is subjectively ordered from the moves I consider to be best to those which are complete and utter rubbish. The latter are among many other openings discussed in my book *Unorthodox Chess Openings*, and will be treated here only when there is an interesting gambit available for White. We'll now turn our attention to those moves worth preparing for.

GAMBITS AGAINST BLACK REPLIES

Let's see what gambits we can use to counter Black's plans.

Black Replies 1...e5

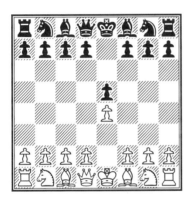

Against 1...e5

The classical defense to the King's Pawn opening invites various gambits. We'll go for the jugular with the ultra-sharp **Göring Gambit**.

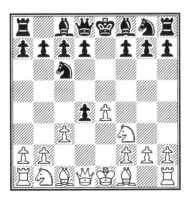

Goring Gambit
1.e4   e5
2.d4   exd4
3.Nf3   Nc6
4.c3

This is a gambit along traditional lines. White gives up the d-pawn in order to accelerate development. Although Black can achieve equality with accurate play, the slightest slip invites disaster.

Our treatment here is different from many books, as I had an opportunity to review and reconsider existing analysis when writing *How to Play the Göring Gambit.* In these sections I share some new secrets with you, moves I found after my monograph went to press.

Black Replies 1...e6

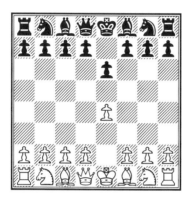

Against 1...e6

The French Defense is popular and leads to solid positions.

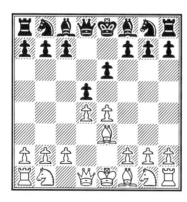

Alapin Gambit
1.e4   e6
2.d4   d5
3.Be3

The **Alapin Gambit** is based on the idea of rapid development while keeping the central post at d4 well protected. Although it is not seen at professional levels of play where defensive technique is taken for granted, it is a very dangerous weapon in the amateur ranks. The mild mannered Rev. Tim Sawyer is an authority on this vicious line, and his book, listed in the bibliography, makes excellent supplemental reading to what I provide here.

Black Replies 1...c5

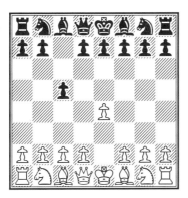

Against 1...c5

Against the Sicilian Defense, White usually reserves sacrifices for the middlegame. The major exception is the immediate offer of the d-pawn, with the Smith-Morra Gambit.

After the moves, 2.d4 cxd4, your opponent is likely to be fully prepared for the Smith-Morra Gambit with 3.c3. That would be an obvious choice for our repertoire, except that to discuss it in any detail would require a book unto itself. Indeed, there is a large and excellent literature devoted to that opening, and you can find references to them in the bibliography.

But for our purposes, let's step a little further off the beaten track for the neglected **Halasz Gambit**.

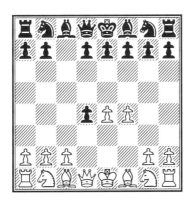

Halasz Gambit
1.e4   c5
2.d4   cxd4
3.f4

3.f4!? Black can try to hold on to the pawn, but that is dangerous. 3...Nc6 is the most logical reply. After 4.Nf3, the only way to hang on to the pawn is 4...Qb6, but even if Black offers to return the pawn instead, White can try other gambit means as we will see.

Black Replies 1...c6

Against 1...c6

The Caro-Kann has a reputation for being a bit boring, but we are going to lively up the scene with an interesting gambit which is often seen in the island paradise of Hawaii - the **Ulysses Gambit**.

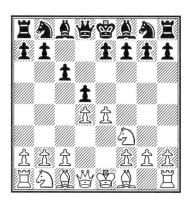

Ulysses Gambit
1.e4   c6
2.d4   d5
3.Nf3

The Ulysses Gambit is rather cunning, and it is not surprising that it has gained a following recently, because strategically, it is quite similar to a popular variation in the main lines. After 3...dxe4; 4.Ng5 we see a resemblance to the new main line in the Karpov Variation: 1.e4 c6; 2.d4 d5; 3.Nc3 exd4; 4.Nxe4 Nd7; 5.Ng5!? which was a mere footnote until the late 1980s.

Black Replies 1...d6

Against 1...d6

This comes in two flavors both starting with 2.d4. This modest advance of the d-pawn can be the prelude to all sorts of defenses. Against 2.Nf3, for example, Black can choose a Sicilian (2...c5), Philidor (2...e5), Modern (2...g6), Pirc (2...Nf6), Czech (2...c6 or 2...Nf6 3.Nc3 c6), St. George (2...a6) or even the shoddy Balogh (2...f5?).

White limits the options somewhat by playing the correct move 2.d4, setting up the ideal pawn center. Black will then choose between the plans involving kingisde fianchetto (Pirc, Modern or Lizard Defenses) or the stodgy Czech Defense. Black can also pick up the St. George with 2...a6, but the pawn on d6 is not part of the standard strategy there.

Let's start with the fianchetto plans, which come in two flavors, both starting with 2.d4.

A) 2...Nf6; 3.Nc3 g6 is the **Pirc Defense**. The variation (3...c6, the Czech Defense, will be met vigorously by 4.f4!) 4.Bc4 Bg7; 5.Qe2 Nc6; 6.e5 involves a gambit of the d-pawn, though Black would do better to decline the bait at d4. 6...Nxd4; 7.exf6 Nxe2; 8.fxg7 Rg8; 9.Ngxe2 Rxg7 gives us three pieces for a queen and two pawns.

That qualifies as a gambit!

B) 2...g6 is the **Lizard**, or the **Modern Defense**.

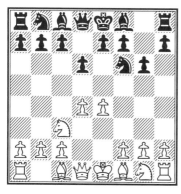

Pirc Defense
1.e4   d6
2.d4   Nf6
3.Nc3   g6

Modern Defense
1.e4   d6
2.d4   g6

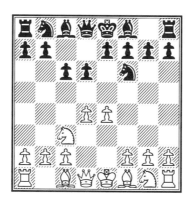

Czech Defense
1.e4   d6
2.d4   Nf6
3.Nc3   c6

It is hard to offer a gambit against the Modern Defense, because Black is hiding out on the back three ranks. But there is one gambit approach which has been seen even in the games of top players. We will develop our bishop at c4, and queen at e2, allowing our opponents to capture our d-pawn with ...Nc6 and ...Nxd4, if they dare!

Black Replies 1...Nf6

Against 1...Nf6

The Alekhine Defense attacks our pawn at e4, but we can gambit it with 2.Bc4, the **Krejcik Variation**, since 2...Nxe4; 3.Bxf7+! Kxf7; 4.Qh5+ lets White recover the piece.

Krejcik Variation
1.e4   Nf6
2.Bc4

Black Replies 1...Nc6

The **Nimzowitsch Defense** can be handled in four quite different fashions after 2.d4, not all of which allow gambit play. 2...e5, however, leads us back to the Göring Gambit after 3.Nf3 exd4; 4.c3. We will look at the gambit variations for this line, of course, under the Göring Gambit.

Black Replies 1...d5

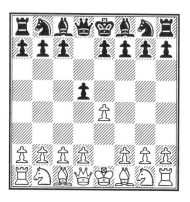

Against 1...d5

One of the really frustrating things about the Scandinavian Defense is that there are no *good* gambits against it, and in fact, it is Black who often gambits the d-pawn, as seen in the companion volume, *Gambit Opening Repertoire for Black.* It doesn't take a rocket scientist to figure out that in any repertoire, there must be at least one position which you have to play for both sides.

If I knew a really effective line against this opening, I would have had to abandon it as the cornerstone of the Black repertoire. So here is my advice: play the normal lines and forget about gambits. Still, since it is easier for White to get away with a dubious gambit than it is for Black, I'll do my best to put a smiley face on the **Tennison Gambit**, 2.Nf3 dxe4, even though I criticize it elsewhere. You can have fun with it in amateur games, if you wish.

Tennison Gambit
1.e4   d5
2.Nf3   dxe4

What can be done about people who decline such gambits? Cowardice used to be punishable by death and dishonor. In chess, all you can do is sigh and try to pound the opponent into submission as quickly as possible.

Black Replies 1...b6

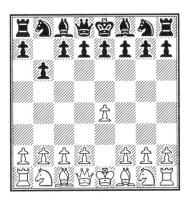

Against 1...b6

The move order, 1...b6, 2.d4 Bb7, is the disreputable **Owen Defense**, and we'll have a bit a fun with it, even though very few players are willing to risk it as Black these days.

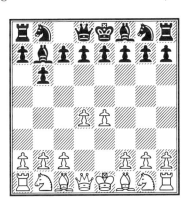

Owen Defense
1.e4   b6
2.d4   Bb7

Other Black Replies

Other moves are sufficiently bad that you can get a good advantage with normal development, and there is no need to sacrifice a pawn in the opening. You can find discussion of some wild gambit ideas in *Unorthodox Chess Openings* but there is no need for special preparation for these rarely encountered deviations.

GÖRING GAMBIT ACCEPTED
• Introduction •

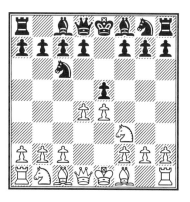

OPENING MOVES

1.e4   e5
2.Nf3   Nc6
3.d4

OVERVIEW

In the main lines of the King Pawn Game, White can try many exciting gambits. We want to play something really aggressive, and get to work on the vulnerable f7-square. If we can get there, a knock-out blow can be delivered.

Fortunately, there is an excellent gambit which can lead to some great attacking chess! The **Göring Gambit** is an old fashioned opening which is once again becoming popular as modern players continue to refurbish ancient lines for use in contemporary tournaments.

The opening starts out with the same moves as the Scotch Game and Scotch Gambit, with White offering a pawn at d4. Black will almost always capture at d4 in this position, because all alternatives are weak. Nevertheless, you can try the more direct move order with 1.e4 e5; 2.d4!?, since after 2...exd4; 3.Nf3, Black almost always plays 3...Nc6, there being no superior move.

GÖRING GAMBIT
Introduction

3...exd4; 4.c3 Nf6	
Options at move 4	24
Option 1: 4...Bc5	24
Option 2: 4...Qe7	25
Option 3: 4...Nge7	26
Option 4: 4...d3	27
5.e5 Ne4	
Options at move 5	30
Option 1: 5...Nd5!?	30
Option 2: 5...Ng8	31
Option 3: 5...Ng4	32
Option 4: 5...Qe7	33

3...exd4; 4.c3.

With this move you put the question to the pawn at d4. Black cannot allow you to simply capture it for free, because then you would have an ideal pawn center which is easy to support. Therefore, Black must choose one of three plans. The pawn at c3 can be captured, though this accelerates White's development. We'll examine that plan in the **Göring Gambit Accepted, Part I**.

The two other main plans involve undermining White's pawn at e4. Black can attack it with a pawn by playing 4...d5, and this is the subject of the **Göring Gambit Declined** chapter. All other alternatives, including the developing move 4...Nf6 which also attacks the pawn, are discussed here.

4...Nf6.

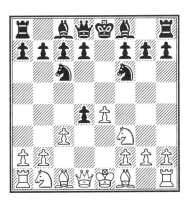

I rather like this plan for Black. It is not without risk, but the rewards can be great. Still, it should not discourage anyone from playing the gambit as White.

Black has other moves here, but they are not very impressive. The pawn at d4 can receive additional support from a bishop at c5, but it isn't enough. Black can try to put pressure on the e-file with ...Qe7, at the cost of locking in the bishop at f8. The odd development of the knight from g8 to e7 has a similar drawback. 4...d3 is abject cowardice! Black simply returns the pawn for no value, and White claims an advantage immediately.

GÖRING GAMBIT - OPTIONS AT MOVE 4

<u>1. e4 e5; 2.Nf3 Nc6; 3.d4 exd4; 4.c3</u>
Option 1: 4... Bc5
Option 2: 4... Qe7
Option 3: 4... Nge7
Option 4: 4... d3

GÖRING GAMBIT, MOVE 4
Option 1: 4...Bc5

This move does not have much of a point, since White can just capture the pawn with an ideal pawn center.

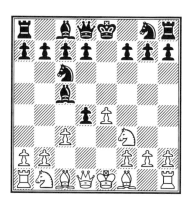

5.cxd4 Bb6; 6.Bc4 d6; 7.Ng5. This is a rather forcing move but it seems to work out well.

A) 7...Bxd4; 8.Bxf7+ Kf8; 9.Bxg8 Rxg8; (9...Kxg8; 10.Qb3+ d5; 11.exd5 Na5; 12.Qa4 c5; 13.dxc6 Nxc6; 14.Qc4+ and White wins.) 10.Nxh7+ is clearly better for White.

B) 7...Nh6; 8.0-0 0-0; 9.Be3!? This introduces complications which turn out to be favorable for White, but Black's position was already bad. 9...Bxd4; 10.Nxf7! Nxf7; 11.Bxd4 Nxd4; 12.Qxd4.

Material is equal, but Black has problems developing. Perhaps moving the king to h8 would be best here. 12...c5; 13.Qd5 Qf6; 14.Nc3 Re8; 15.Rad1 Be6; 16.Qd3 Ne5. This looks powerful, but in fact it leads to a lost position. 17.Bxe6+ Rxe6; 18.Qd5 Rae8; 19.f4! Nf7; 20.Qxb7. Black is busted.

White's control of the center provided all that was needed to obtain a material advantage. 20...g6; 21.Qxa7 h5; 22.e5 Qf5; 23.Nd5 Nh6; 24.Nf6+ Rxf6; 25.exf6 Qxf6; 26.Qd7 Re6; 27.a4 Nf5; 28.Rfe1 Ne3; 29.Rd3 and White won, Lord – Thomas, Postal 1986.

GÖRING GAMBIT, MOVE 4
Option 2: 4...Qe7

A move that places the queen on a bad square, and she will have to move again soon.

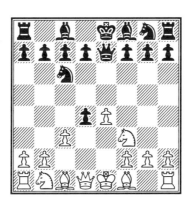

5.Bd3 d5; 6.0-0 dxe4; 7.Bxe4 Qd6; 8.Re1 Be6; 9.Bxc6+ Qxc6; 10.Nxd4 Qd7; 11.Nxe6 fxe6; 12.Qh5+ g6; 13.Qe5 Bg7; 14.Qxe6+ Qxe6; 15.Rxe6+ and White held a large advantage in Michalek – Cejkova, Czechoslovakia 1992.

GÖRING GAMBIT, MOVE 4
Option 3: 4...Nge7

This is another unusual defense, but it is not at all bad.

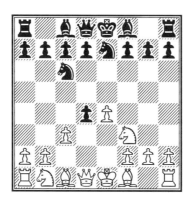

5.Bc4 is now met by **5...d5!** This move frees Black's game. **6.exd5 Nxd5; 7.0-0 Be7;** (7...Nb6; 8.Bb5 dxc3; 9.Qxd8+ Kxd8; 10.Bxc6 bxc6; 11.Ne5 Be6; 12.Nxc6+ Kc8; 13.Nxc3 is a bit better for White. The Black king may find itself in danger on the queenside.) **8.Qb3** and now:

A) 8...Na5; 9.Qa4+ c6; 10.Bxd5 Qxd5 was seen in Chesca – Ciocaltea, Rumania 1975, but now 11.cxd4 is slightly better for White, according to the *Encyclopedia of Chess Openings*. I doubt that. Black has the bishop pair and better pawn structure, and only needs to deal with the problem of the knight at a5. 11...0-0; 12.Nc3 Qh5; 13.Bd2 (13.Ne5 Bd8; 14.b4 f6 leads to interesting complications–Magar.) 13...Be6; 14.b3 (14.d5 Bxd5; 15.Qxa5 Bxf3 is clearly better for Black.) 14...Bd8! and Black has a good game.

B) 8...Be6 is a much better move than 8...Na5. 9.Nxd4 Nxd4; 10.cxd4 0-0 and here 11.Qxb7 Bf6; 12.Rd1 Qd6 is interesting. Does Black have enough for the pawn?

GÖRING GAMBIT, MOVE 4
Option 4: 4...d3

As we have already noted, this move is a timid reaction.

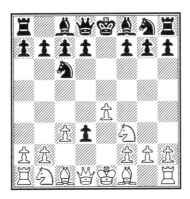

After **5.Bxc4 Bc5** we reach the following position.

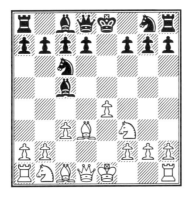

This is a logical method of development. Black takes aim at f2 and would like to play ...Nf6 and ...Ng4, or just develop with ...d6 and kingside castling.

6.0–0 d6.

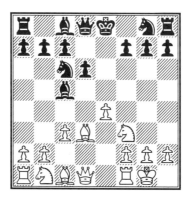

White has tried many moves here. **7.Nbd2 a5** (7...a6; 8.Nc4 Nge7 9.a4 a5; 10.Be3 Bxe3; 11.Nxe3 was a little better for White in Illescas – Eslon, Spain 1984, but Black should not have gone in for 11...Ne5?!) **8.Re1 Nge7; 9.Nf1 0–0; 10.Be3 Bxe3; 11.Nxe3 Ng6; 12.Bc2.** This position was also reached in Penrose – Keres, Moscow (Olympiad) 1956. **12...Be6** was greeted by **13.Nd4!**

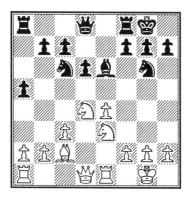

Now Black must choose between giving White an ideal pawn center or allowing infiltration at f5. **13...Bd7** (13...Nxd4; 14.cxd4 and the f-pawn will start marching soon.) **14.Ndf5 Qg5?** This just wastes time. **15.g3 Qd8; 16.Qh5 f6; 17.f4** and White went on to win in Przybyla – Kolmann, Postal 1992.

Alternatively, Black can try **5...d6.** Here **6.h3!** is generally considered best. **6...Nf6; 7.0–0 Be7.** Such solid setups are often seen, but Black lacks sufficient room to maneuver. **8.Nd4 0–0.**

9.Nd2 Re8. This is the only sensible move. The knight at c6 should stay in place. Black employs a standard defensive plan in the Open Games. Continuing with ...Bf8, ...g6, and ...Bg7. 9...Ne5; 10.Bc2 c5; 11.Nf5 Bxf5; 12.exf5 d5; 13.g4 leads to an exciting game. For example, 13...Nc6; 14.g5 Ne8; 15.f6 Bd6; 16.Qh5 g6; 17.Qh6 Bf4; 18.Nf3 Qd6; 19.Nh4 Nxf6; 20.Bxf4 Qxf4; 21.Ng2 Sermek – Scetinin, 1992. **10.f4 Bf8!** The alternative plan with 10...Nd7; 11.N2f3 Bf6; 12.Be3 g6; 13.Qc2 Bg7; 14.Rae1 Nxd4; 15.cxd4 gave White a clear advantage in Velimirovic – Ivkov, Skopje 1976, but the error was in the capture at d4 by Black. **11.Qc2 g6; 12.N2f3 Bg7.** 12...Nd7; 13.Bc4 Nb6; 14.Bd3 Nb8 is a strange plan, and after 15.f5! White had the advantage in Velimirovic – Donner, The Hague (Zonal) 1966. **13.Bd2 Bd7; 14.Rae1 Qe7.** 14...a6 is playable, for example 15.Ng5 Re7; 16.e5 dxe5; 17.Nxc6 Bxc6; 18.fxe5 Qd5; 19.Nf3 Nd7; 20.c4 Qc5+; 21.Be3 Qa5; 22.Bd2 Qd5 was agreed drawn in Velimirovic – Keres, Sukhumi 1966. **15.a3 a6; 16.b4** with a dynamic game, Ciocaltea – Gheorghiu, Rumanian Championship.

Returning to the Main Line

Let's return to the main line after 4...Nf6. Now White takes the initiative by advancing in the center.

5.e5.

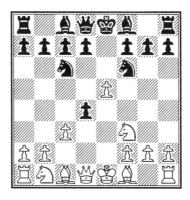

5...Ne4. This is the typical plan in the double king pawn game when White advances to e5. Once again, we have four alternatives to consider. The knight can take up a post at d5, though it can be vulnerable there. Retreating to g8, on the other hand, leaves Black severely behind in development. Leaping to g4 has its risks, too. Finally, there is again the option of placing the queen at e7, but that really screws up Black's development.

GÖRING GAMBIT - OPTIONS AT MOVE 5
1.e4 e5; 2.Nf3 Nc6; 3.d4 exd4; 4.c3 Nf6; 5.e5
Option 1: 5...Nd5
Option 2: 5...Ng8
Option 3: 5...Ng4

GÖRING GAMBIT, MOVE 5
Option 1: 5...Nd5!?
This Alekhinish move is not even mentioned in early sources, but it has found some followers recently.

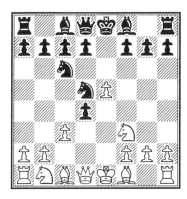

6.cxd4 d6 is the popular line (6...Bb4+; 7.Bd2 Bxd2+; 8.Qxd2 d6; 9.Nc3 Nxc3; 10.Qxc3 was better for White in Sermek – I. Sokolov, Portoroz 1993.) and now White continues 7.Bb5 with two possibilities.

A) 7...Be7; 8.Nc3 Nxc3; 9.bxc3 0–0; 10.0–0 Bg4; (10...Bf5; 11.Re1 was just a little better for White in Deyev – Goldin, Podolsk 1990.) 11.Qd3 Qc8; 12.Bf4 Qf5; 13.Qxf5 Bxf5; 14.Rfe1 d5; 15.Bg5 Bxg5; 16.Nxg5 h6; 17.Nf3 Nd8; 18.Nh4 Bh7; 19.f4 c6; 20.Bf1 g5; 21.fxg5 hxg5; 22.Nf3 was better for White in Lukin – Tseshkovsky, Russian Championship 1995.

B) 7...dxe5!? is probably stronger. 8.Nxe5 Bb4+; 9.Bd2 0–0; 10.Bxc6 bxc6; 11.0–0 and here I can't believe that 11...Bd6; 12.Nxc6 Qh4; 13.g3 Qh3 gives Black enough for the pawn after 14.Qf3 as in Neumeier – Klinger, Vienna 1988.

GÖRING GAMBIT, MOVE 5
Option 2: 5...Ng8

The retreat of the knight is usually rejected summarily on the basis of one old game, but it seems unlikely that Black can afford to waste two tempi just to draw the pawn to e5.

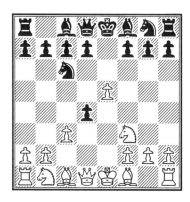

6.Bc4 d5; 7.exd6 Bxd6; 8.0-0 Nf6; 9.Re1+ Be7. Black has wasted an enormous amount of time yet is not far behind in development, and the position seems playable. 10.Bb5 0-0; 11.Bxc6 bxc6; 12.Nxd4 Bd7; 13.Qf3 Re8; 14.Bg5 Rb8 and Black was only a little worse in Mieses – Forgac, German Chess Congress XIV 1904.

GÖRING GAMBIT, MOVE 5
Option 3: 5...Ng4
The knight flees to the kingside.

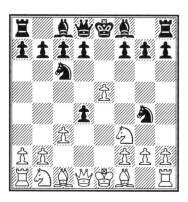

6.cxd4 Nb4 sends the horses out to graze in barren territory. 7.Bc4 Nc6; 8.0-0 Bb4; 9.a3 and White was better in Schiller – Hobart, Internet (ICC) 1996.

GÖRING GAMBIT, MOVE 5
Option 4: 5...Qe7
This is a poor choice, as usual, because it impedes development.

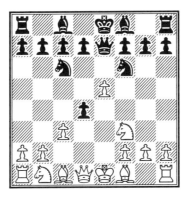

6.cxd4 d6; 7.Bb5 Bd7; 8.0-0 dxe5; 9.Bxc6 Bxc6; 10.Nxe5 Bd7; 11.Re1 Be6; 12.Nc3 0-0-0; 13.Be3 Nd5; 14.Nb5 a6; 15.Na7+. White won. Meek – Fuller, USA Congress 1857.

Returning to the Main Line
So, having rejected the alternatives we return to the main lines with **5...Ne4!**

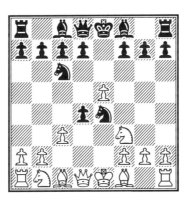

6.Qe2 f5. Supporting the knight with the f-pawn is considered to be the only move, but perhaps 6...d5 deserves further investigation. 6...d5; 7.exd6 f5.

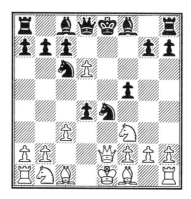

8.Nxd4 Nxd4; 9.cxd4 Bxd6; 10.f3 Qh4+; 11.Kd1! 0-0; 12.fxe4 fxe4; 13.Qc4+. White can also play simply h3, as in Uzman – Bisguier, Norristown 1973. 13...Kh8; 14.Be3 Bxh2; 15.Nc3 Bg4+; 16.Be2 Qg3; 17.Kd2 Bf5; 18.Rhf1 Qxg2; 19.Rf2 and Black's attack had run out of steam. 19...Qg3; 20.Rh1 Bg1; 21.Rxg1 Qxg1; 22.Rxf5 Qh2; 23.Rh5 Qg2; 24.Qxc7 Black resigned, Bazan – Luna, Buenos Aires 1970. **7.exf6.** 7.Nxd4?! runs into 7...Bc5! since 8.Nxf5 0-0; 9.Qxe4 d5; 10.exd6 Bxf2+; 11.Kxf2 Bxf5 wins for Black, according to analysis by Penrose. **7...d5.**

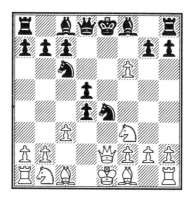

8.Nbd2. Developing seems best. The capture 8.fxg7 Bxg7; 9.Nxd4 0-0 is good for Black, e.g., 10.Be3 Nxd4; 11.cxd4 Nxf2; 12.Bxf2 Re8. Casafus – Boey, Lugano Olympiad 1968. **8...Qxf6.** This is the obvious move, but here 8...d3!? is a secure path to equality.

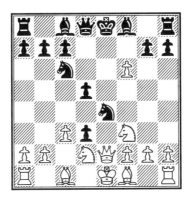

Giving back the pawn lets Black eliminate the pin on the e-file. 9.Qe3 is the best reply, in my opinion.

Now Black plays 9...Bc5! (9...Qxf6; 10.Nxe4 dxe4; 11.Qxe4+ Be7; 12.Bxd3 Be6; 13.0-0 0-0-0 14.Bg5 Qf7; 15.Rfe1 Bf6; 16.Qxe6+ Qxe6; 17.Rxe6 Rxd3; 18.Bxf6 gxf6; 19.Rxf6 with a clear advantage for White in Bryson – Elbilia, Moscow Olympiad 1994.) 10.fxg7 (10.Nd4 Bxd4; 11.cxd4 0-0; 12.fxg7 Re8 was better for Black in Bjorkqvist – Norvama, Postal 1980. White can try exchanging at e4 instead of capturing at g7.) 10...Rg8; 11.Nd4 Bxd4; 12.cxd4 Bf5; 13.Bxd3 Qe7; 14.Bb5 0-0-0 15.Bxc6 bxc6; 16.Nxe4 dxe4; 17.Qc3 was played in Iskov – Kaiszauri, Oslo 1980, but Black seems to have a strong game after 17...e3!; 18.Bxe3 Rxg7.

Now White must improve on 19.Qxc6 Be4; 20.Qc5 Qf7; 21.Rc1 Rxg2 and the game concluded 22.Qe5 Bb7; 23.Rc5 Rg4; 24.f3 Rg2; 25.Bf4 Rd7; 26.Kd1 Bxf3+; 27.Kc1 Rg4; 28.Bg3 Bxh1. White resigned. 19.Rg1 is a move I didn't consider in *How to Play the Göring Gambit*. It looks odd, but may be the best available try. 19...Be4; 20.g3 is ugly, but perhaps the White king is safe enough at e1 or, eventually, at c1. Two pawns are a lot of material!

9.Nxe4.

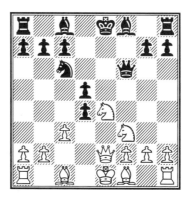

White can also capture the other pawn. 9.Nxd4 Nxd4; 10.cxd4 Qe7; 11.Nxe4 dxe4; 12.a3 Bd7; 13.Bf4 Bc6; 14.Qe3 0-0-0; 15.Bg5 Qd6; 16.Bxd8 Qxd8; 17.d5 Bxd5; 18.0-0-0 Kb8; 19.Bc4 c6; 20.Bxd5 cxd5; 21.Kb1 was clearly better for White in Hagstrom - Englund, Postal 1978. **9...dxe4; 10.Qxe4+ Qe6.** 10...Be7; 11.Bb5 dxc3; 12.0-0 is winning for White, according to Cimmino. This requires some justification. 12...Bf5 (12...cxb2?; 13.Bxc6+ bxc6; 14.Bxb2 Qe6; 15.Qxe6 Bxe6; 16.Rfe1 Kf7; 17.Bxg7 Kxg7; 18.Rxe6 Kf7; 19.Rxc6 is better for White.) 13.Bxc6+ bxc6; 14.Qe2 Rb8! and Black looks fine to me. **11.Bd3.** 11.Qxe6+ Bxe6; 12.cxd4 0-0-0; 13.Be3 Bb4+ gives Black compensation for the pawn. **11...dxc3.** 11...Qxe4+!?; 12.Bxe4 dxc3; 13.0-0 and now 13...Bd6; 14.Re1 0-0; 15.bxc3 Ne7; 16.Bg5 Ng6; 17.Bxg6 hxg6; 18.Be7 gave White the advantage in Shevelev - Bezman, USSR 1989. **12.bxc3 Be7; 13.Bf4 Bf6.** 13...0-0??; 14.Bc4 and Black resigned in Schneider - Kaiszauri, Copenhagen (Rilton Cup) 1980. **14.Kd2 Qxe4; 15.Bxe4 Bd7; 16.Bxc7 Rc8; 17.Bg3.**

White is better, according to analysis by Cimmino. We have seen in the notes that Black has some promising alternatives, and White must be prepared to work hard to justify material sacrifices. Still, the positions allow Black every opportunity to make the kind of small error that will prove fatal.

GÖRING GAMBIT ACCEPTED
• (Part One) •

OPENING MOVES
1.e4   e5
2.Nf3   Nc6
3.d4   exd4
4.c3   dxc3
5.Nxc3

OVERVIEW

When Black accepts the pawn in the Göring Gambit, called the **Göring Gambit Accepted**, sparks can fly on both sides of the board. White has easy development, and the lack of a pawn at c2 has the benefit of allowing the queen to get to a4 or b3 where it can be particularly effective. The open files in the center can be seized quickly, as Black needs time to mobilize.

From Black's point of view, it is important to develop with tempo by creating threats. Black's primary candidate is deploying the bishop at b4, pinning the enemy knight, and reducing its attacking force.

5...Bb4 is the main line. We'll get to that move in the Göring Gambit, Part 3. In this chapter and the next, Part I and Part II, we will examine the alternatives.

There are three options to the main line for Black. Kingside development can be continued by bringing a bishop to c5 or getting the knight to f6. Alternatively, Black can work on the critical e5-square with ...d6. In any case, your attacking opportunities will materialize.

GÖRING GAMBIT
Accepted: Part One

Continuation	
Options at move 5	39
Option 1: 5...Bc5	39
Option 2: 5...Nf6	40
Option 3: 5...d6 (next chapter)	

GÖRING GAMBIT - OPTIONS AT MOVE 5
1.e4 e5; 2.Nf3 Nc6; 3.d4 exd4; 4.c3 dxc3; 5.Nxc3
Option 1: 5...Bc5
Option 2: 5...Nf6
Option 3: 5...d6 (next chapter)

GÖRING GAMBIT, MOVE 5
Option 1: 5...Bc5

This plan may be under-appreciated.

6.Bc4 d6.

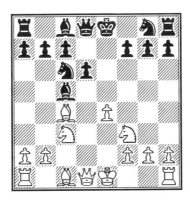

Black sets up a solid position and aims for rapid development.
(6...Nge7; 7.Ng5 Ne5; 8.Nxf7 Nxf7; 9.Bxf7+ Kxf7; 10.Qh5+ g6;

11.Qxc5 is better for White, Siedler – Ruiz, Buenos Aires 1974. Material is equal but the Black king is exposed.) 7.Qb3 (7.e5!? comes into consideration.)

A) 7...Qe7; 8.0-0 gives White a strong threat of Nd5, but Black can play 8...Qd7, admitting the mistake, and although a tempo down, could play on. But of course it is better just to plant the queen at d7 in the first place.(8.0-0 Nf6; 9.Re1 0-0; 10.Bg5 Na5; 11.Qa4 Nxc4; 12.Qxc4 h6; 13.Bh4 Qe6 and Black was just a pawn ahead in Vajdeslaver – Stotzkaya, European Youth Chess 1992.)

B) 7...Qd7!; 8.Nd5 Nge7. Black has nothing to worry about here. 9.Qc3 0-0; 10.Bh6. Described as "a powerful shot" by Smith & Hall, but it falls harmlessly to the ground. 10...Qg4. The bishop could not be captured because of Nf6+, but this move saves the day. 11.Ng5 Bd4!; 12.Nxe7+.

Smith & Hall break off here with the comment that "after 12...Kh8; 13.Qd2 Black is in terrible shape". Maybe so, but there is a much simpler reply: 12...Nxe7! (12...Kh8; 13.Qd3 is good for White, as pointed out by Schwarz 1978.) 13.Qxd4 gxh6. In my opinion, White is worse. Exchanging at f7 is hardly a good idea: 14.Nxf7 (14.Nf3 Be6 is also fine for Black.) 14...Rxf7; 15.Bxf7+ Kxf7; 16.0-0 Be6. Black has two pieces for a rook and a strong attacking position.

GÖRING GAMBIT, MOVE 5
Option 2: 5...Nf6

This is a logical developing move, but White can obtain a strong initiative immediately by attacking the knight.

6.e5! Ng4. Retreating to g8 would leave Black with a terrible position. 7.Qe2. White now threatens h3 followed by Bxh6, so Black has little choice. 7...h5. This is the only consistent follow-up, though it isn't very effective. 8.h3 Nh6; 9.Bf4 Nf5.

White has much greater development and most of the center. By castling, White contests the remaining central square at d4. 10.0–0–0 g6. Now there is a new hole beckoning at f6. 11.Nd5 Bh6; 12.Nf6+ Kf8; 13.Ng5 Qe7; 14.g4! White's attack is relentless, and Black still has no counterplay. 14...Nfd4; 15.Qe4 Qc5+; 16.Kb1 Bxg5! (16...d6; 17.Rc1 Qa5; 18.Nxf7 Kxf7; 19.Bc4+ Kf8; 20.Qxg6 and White wins. The knight at g5 is too powerful, and must be eliminated.) 17.Bxg5 and White has a powerful position, Clarke – Sofrigin, Lyngby 1990.

GÖRING GAMBIT ACCEPTED
(Part Two)

OPENING MOVES	
1.e4	e5
2.Nf3	Nc6
3.d4	exd4
4.c3	dxc3
5.Nxc3	d6
6.Bc4	

OVERVIEW

This line of the **Göring Gambit Accepted**, including White's bishop move to c4 on the sixth move, and Black's response, is what we'll examine in this chapter. Black has played 5...d6, the third option we mentioned last chapter, and we respond with the normal move, 6.Bc4. This is a sensible continuation for both sides. Black opens a line for the bishop at c8, even if it does rather limit the options for his fellow cleric, who must now head to e7, or, in some circumstances, to g7. White will maintain an advantage in space, but after all, a pawn has been invested to get it.

The question now is whether Black can afford to play 6...Be6. This offers an exchange which will damage Black's pawn structure, at least temporarily. It seems that this line is fine for Black.

We'll take a look at the critical plan where White will exchange bishops immediately at e6. We'll also take a look at 6...Be7, which is a more conservative move, and 6...Nf6, which can lead to very sharp play.

GÖRING GAMBIT	
Accepted: Part Two	
Continuation	
Options at move 6	43
Option 1: 6...Be7	43
Option 2: 6...Nf6	45
Option 3: 6...Be6	52

GÖRING GAMBIT - OPTIONS AT MOVE 6

1.e4 e5; 2.Nf3 Nc6; 3.d4 exd4; 4.c3 dxc3; 5.Nxc3 d6; 6.Bc4
Option 1: 6...Be7
Option 2: 6...Nf6
Option 3: 6...Be6

GÖRING GAMBIT, MOVE 6
Option 1: 6...Be7

As is so often the case in the Göring, this simple developing move fails because White can set up the powerful battery of queen and bishop on the a2–g8 diagonal, and win the pawn at f7.

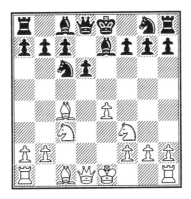

7.Qb3. 7...Be6 does not work here. 8.Bxe6 (8.Qxb7 Na5; 9.Bb5+ Kf8; 10.Qa6 is an alternative, Chersich – Matsuo, World Junior Championship 1995) 8...fxe6; 9.Qxb7 Na5; 10.Qa6 c6; (10...c5; 11.Qb5+ Kf7; 12.0-0 Rb8; 13.Qe2 leaves Black with the difficult question of how to develop the knight from g8.) 11.b4 Bf6; 12.e5! dxe5; 13.bxa5 and White wins.

7...Na5; 8.Bxf7+ Kf8; 9.Qa4.

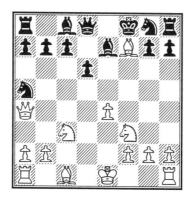

Black has to capture at f7 now, because 9...c6; 10.Bxg8 Kxg8; (10...Rxg8; 11.0-0 Be6; 12.Bf4 b5; 13.Qc2 g5; 14.Bg3 Rg6; 15.Rfd1 and in Probik – Michalek, Postal 1985, White regained the d-pawn with a clear advantage.) leaves Black in trouble, for example, 11.0-0 b5; (11...Kf7; 12.e5 Re8; 13.exd6 Bxd6; 14.Rd1 is given by Smith & Hall. The Black queen is overworked trying to defend the knight at a5 and bishop at d6.) 12.Qc2 Bg4; 13.Nd4 Bf6; 14.Be3. Black's pieces are a mess, and White is not even down a pawn! 14...Qe8; 15.f3 Bd7; 16.Rad1 Nc4; 17.Bc1 Qe5; 18.b3 Nb6; 19.Nce2 c5; 20.f4 Qe7; 21.Nf3 and White can look forward to victory.

9...Kxf7; 10.Qxa5 is more common.

Advancing the c-pawn is commonly seen to keep the enemy knight off of d5 or b5.

10...c6. After 10...Be6; 11.0-0 White has some compensation, though it is not clear that it is enough. 11...Kf8? (11...c5 is an obvious improvement, and Black's position is not so bad.) 12.Nd5.

It is no fun to play such positions as Black when you are facing Mikhail Tal! 12...c6; 13.Nc7 Bf7; 14.Nd4 Qc8; 15.Nxa8 Qxa8; 16.Nf5 b6; 17.Qc3 Bf6; 18.Qg3 Ne7; 19.Qxd6 Ke8; 20.Bh6 Rg8; 21.Rad1 Qc8; 22.Bxg7 Nxf5; 23.exf5 Be7; 24.Rfe1 Be6; 25.Rxe6 Rxg7; 26.f6. White won. Tal – Russell, Munich Olympiad 1958.

11.Qxd8 Bxd8; 12.Bf4.

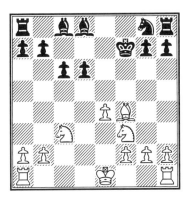

12...Ke7 (12...Nf6; 13.Bxd6 and White is simply a pawn ahead in an endgame, Pribik – Batik, Postal 1984). **13.0–0–0 Bc7; 14.e5! d5.**

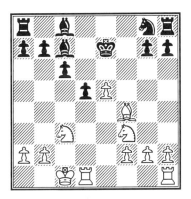

White now wins with a nice combination, based on use of the d5-square. **15.Rxd5 cxd5; 16.Nxd5+ Kd7; 17.e6+ Kxe6; 18.Nxc7+ Kf5; 19.Be5** and Black gave up, Bryson – Thipsay, British Championship 1985.

GÖRING GAMBIT, MOVE 6
Option 2: 6...Nf6.

This is a simple developing move.

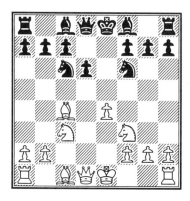

White should add some pressure with **7.Qb3.** After all, we don't want Black to become too comfortable!

Now we are into one of the main lines of the Göring Gambit. It turns out, however, that if one cuts through the jungle of variations, it becomes clear that Black is doing fine. Finding the correct moves is not really so difficult, as long as one pays attention to the various threats.

7...Qd7. An awkward move but it seems essential. **8.Ng5.** This is the logical continuation for White. 8.Nd5 Na5; 9.Nxf6+ gxf6; 10.Qc3 Nxc4; 11.Qxc4 Rg8; 12.Bf4 Qg4; 13.Bg3 f5 was good for Black in Ezsol – Horvath, Hungary 1993, while 8.Qc2 Ne5; 9.Nxe5 dxe5; 10.0-0 Bc5; 11.Bg5 c6; 12.h3 Qe7; 13.a3 0-0; 14.b4 Bd4 and Black was clearly better in Zabala – Perez, Spain 1993.

8...Ne5. Black defends f7 while attacking the bishop at c4.

9.Bb5. Clearly the best plan, forcing Black to weaken the queenside pawn structure. **9...c6.**

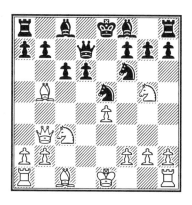

Now things get complicated after **10.f4!** There are a number of plans we must consider. Let's not waste much time on 10...h6? because after 11.fxe5 hxg5; 12.exf6 cxb5; 13.0-0 gxf6; 14.Nd5 Bg7; 15.Nxf6+ Bxf6; 16.Rxf6, White was much better in Svatos – Jerabek, Czechia 1993. That leaves moving the knight to g4, or capturing the bishop at b5. The latter requires more guts, but is probably best.

A) **10...Neg4!?**

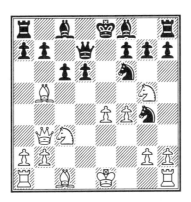

This is better than Smith & Hall indicate in their book on the gambit, and may be a worthy alternative to capturing at b5. 11.Be2! is best, I think. 11...h6 (11...d5 is worth looking at. 12.h3 Nh6; 13.e5 Ne4; 14.Ncxe4 dxe4; 15.Be3 Be7; 16.Rd1 Qc7; 17.Bc4 0-0; 18.0-0 b5; 19.Be2 Nf5; 20.Nxe4 Be6; 21.Qc3 b4; 22.Qc1 Bd5; 23.Bf3 Nxe3; 24.Qxe3 Qb6; 25.Qf2 Rfd8; 26.Rc1 Rac8; 27.b3 Bh4; 28.Qc5 Be7; 29.Qf2 was agreed drawn in Minguell – Fernandez, Barcelona 1986.) 12.Nf3.

This is an important position. I don't think that Black can equalize. 12...d5 (12...Nh5?; 13.0–0 g6; 14.Bc4 d5; 15.exd5 Bc5+; 16.Kh1 Nf2+; 17.Rxf2 Bxf2; 18.dxc6 bxc6; 19.Ne5 was crushing in Schoppmeier – Schlotthauber, Postal 1987. Try naming that game quickly three times, and then forgive me for describing the course of the game as rather "schloppy".) Now White gets nowhere by advancing, for example 13.e5 Ne4; 14.Nd4 Qd8; 15.Nxe4 dxe4; 16.Be3 Bb4+; 17.Kf1 Nxe3+; 18.Qxe3 Bc5; 19.Rd1 Bxd4; 20.Rxd4 Qb6; 21.b3 0–0; 22.Kf2 Be6; 23.Qxe4 f6; 24.Rhd1 Bd5.

But there is a much stronger move: 13.h3!

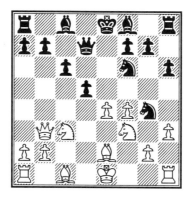

Now 13...d4 is a mistake: 14.hxg4 dxc3; 15.Ne5 Qe7; 16.Bc4 Be6; 17.Bxe6 fxe6; 18.bxc3 is the result of lengthy analytical excursions by B.H. Wood and George Botterill. White is clearly better, with a promising attack. But I think that Smith & Hall really overestimate 13...dxe4, because they do not examine 14.Ng1!? After all, the knight at g4 has no retreat and now the plan seen against the alternative move to h4 does not work. 14...Nf2; 15.Kxf2 Bc5+; 16.Be3 Bxe3+; 17.Kxe3 and the White king is perfectly safe.

B) **10...cxb5!; 11.fxe5.**

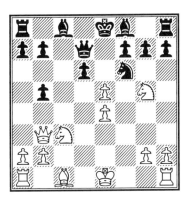

If 11...Ng4, 12.e6! is the correct move, and this effectively refutes Black's plan. 12...fxe6 is forced.

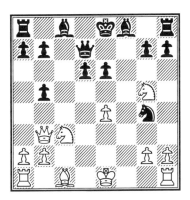

13.Nxb5 a6. (13...Qc6 is given by Smith & Hall, but it doesn't lead to equality. 14.Nd4 Qb6; 15.Ngxe6 Qxb3; 16.axb3 Bxe6; 17.Nxe6 looks a bit better for White.) 14.Nd4 e5; 15.Nde6 was better for White in Coleman – Gretarsson, Postal 1995.

So we will concentrate on **11...dxe5; 12.Be3.**

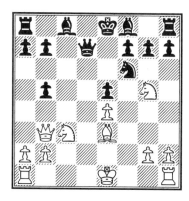

This is the critical position. After many years of analysis, there is a consensus that Black's best plan is to advance the a-pawn and get something going on the queenside. **12...a5!** This relatively quiet move saves Black. But we must examine the alternatives.

12...h6; 13.Rd1 Qe7; 14.Bc5 Qc7; 15.Nxb5 Qa5+; 16.Kf1 hxg5; 17.Qa4 forced Black to resign in Chudinovsky – Nogovitsyn, USSR Championship 1964.

Nor is their any relief after 12...b4? as Black tries to take the initiative, but it does not work. 13.Rd1 Qe7; 14.Nb5 Be6; 15.Nxe6. Black resigned in Smederevac – Tomsic, Yugoslav Championship 1957.

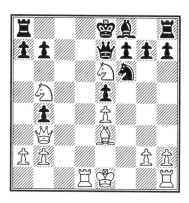

There is no defense to the combined threats at d6, c7, and e6.

12...Bd6 (12...a6? is the sort of time–wasting move Black simply cannot afford. 13.Rd1 Qc7; 14.Bb6 Qc4; 15.Rd8+ Ke7; 16.Qd1 Qc6; 17.Re8+. White won, Hall – Lambers, England 1969.)13.Nxb5 0–0; 14.Rd1 Ne8; 15.Nxd6 Nxd6; 16.Bc5 Qg4; 17.Bxd6 Qxg5; 18.Bxf8

Qxg2; 19.Qg3! Qxe4+; 20.Kf2 Qc2+?!; 21.Ke3 Kxf8; 22.Qxe5+ – and White was winning in Fortes – Seba, World Under–18 Championship 1993.) 13.0-0 a4; 14.Qxb5.

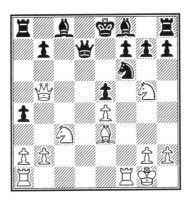

14...Be7! (14...Bd6?; 15.Qe2 0-0; 16.Rxf6 gxf6; 17.Nxh7 Kxh7; 18.Qh5+ Kg8; 19.Nd5 Be7; 20.Rf1 is a convincing line from John Hall.) 15.Qxe5 (15.Rad1 Qxb5; 16.Nxb5 0-0; 17.Nc7 Bg4 and Black is fine, according to Smith & Hall. 15.Bc5 Bxc5+; 16.Qxc5 Qc6 is not a problem either.) 15...0-0!; 16.Rad1 Qe8; 17.Bc5 Bxc5+; 18.Qxc5 Qc6; 19.Qxc6 bxc6; 20.Rd6 Ra5; 21.Nf3 Bb7; 22.Nd4 and White was better in Prates – Van Riemsdijk, Brazilian Championship 1995.

GÖRING GAMBIT, MOVE 6
Option 3: 6...Be6

White gladly accepts the offer to exchange bishops and weaken the forecourt of the enemy king. **7.Bxe6 fxe6; 8.Qb3.**

Here I prefer the solid 8...Qc8 to 8...Qd7, though both moves seem to give Black a playable game. Nevertheless, you are likely to run into both moves. First we will look at the latter move, then move on to the more complicated topic of the retreat to c8.

8...Qd7 can lead to very exciting play. 9.Qxb7 Rb8; 10.Qa6 Be7; 11.0-0 is the normal continuation.

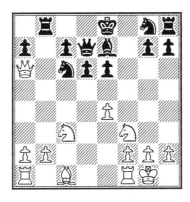

Now the question is, which piece should go to f6? I think Black is in trouble either way. 11...Bf6?!; 12.Rd1 Nge7; 13.Qe2 0-0; 14.e5! Nxe5; 15.Nxe5 Qc8; 16.Ng4 Bxc3; 17.bxc3 gave White a winning position in Smith – Bisguier, Sparks 1970. On the other hand, 11...Nf6; 12.Rd1 0-0; 13.Qe2 e5; 14.Nd5 Nxd5 (14...Rbe8; 15.Bg5 h6; 16.Bxf6 Bxf6; 17.Rac1 won for White in Boesenberg – Geisler, Postal 1989.) 15.exd5 Nd8; 16.Be3 c5; 17.dxc6 Nxc6; 18.Rac1 Kh8; 19.b3 Qb7; 20.Ng5 Nd4; 21.Qd3 Nf5; 22.Ne4 g6; 23.Nc3 Nh4; 24.Nd5 Bd8; 25.f4 exf4; 26.Bxf4 Bb6+; 27.Kh1 Nxg2; 28.Bh6 and Black resigned in Klovan – Tolusch, Riga 1962.

So let's turn now to **8...Qc8; 9.Ng5 Nd8.**

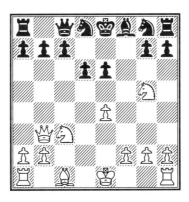

White has invested a pawn, and has some compensation in that Black has no development at all. If Black is given sufficient time, however, development will take place and White will have nothing to show for the material.

10.f4 is the reply, with two important variations.

A) 10...h6; 11.Nf3. Black has tried three reasonable plans here, but all have gone down to defeat!

A1) 11...Ne7; 12.0-0 Nec6; 13.Nh4 Be7; 14.Ng6 Rg8 and now 15.f5 Bf6; 16.Be3 Qd7; 17.Nf4 Nd4; 18.fxe6 Qxe6; 19.Nxe6 Nxb3; 20.Nxc7+ Kd7; 21.axb3 Kxc7; 22.Nd5+ Kd7; 23.Rxf6! forced Black's capitulation in Bonner – Sacarello, Siegen 1970.

A2) 11...c6; 12.Nh4 Ne7; 13.f5 g5?! (13...d5!? is possible but not 13...exf5; 14.exf5 Nxf5; 15.Ng6 and White wins.) 14.fxg6 Rg8; 15.Qd1 Kd7; 16.0-0. White is better and went on to win: 16...Bg7; 17.Bf4 Qc7; 18.Kh1 Rf8; 19.Rc1 a6; 20.Na4 e5; 21.Qg4+ Ke8; 22.Be3 b5; 23.Rxf8+ Kxf8; 24.Nb6 Ra7; 25.Nd5! Nxd5; 26.exd5 Ra8; 27.dxc6 Rc8; 28.Bb6. Black resigned, Espinosa – Vila Sala, Postal 1988.

A3) 11...Nf6; 12.Nh4 Qd7; 13.Ng6 Rg8; 14.e5 dxe5; 15.Nxe5 Qd4; 16.Bd2 Ne4; 17.0-0-0 Nxd2; 18.Rxd2 Qxf4; 19.Qb5+ c6; 20.Qd3 and Black resigned in Tseitlin – Pimonov, USSR Club Championship 1971.

So it seems that Black cannot get away with ...h6. Now let us see what happens with the better defense:

B) **10...Be7!** Failure to attend to development can prove fatal, as we have seen. Now White plays **11.f5!** This forces Black to make an immediate and important decision. The pawn can be captured, ignored, or bypassed. It is this last choice which gives Black the best chance to come out of the opening alive.

Again there are three important paths. The e-pawn can advance in the center, getting out of danger. Black can also capture the invading knight or pawn.

B1) **11...e5!**

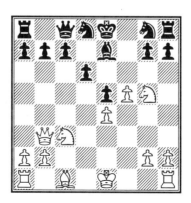

This is the best move. 12.0-0 h6 (12...Nf6; 13.Be3 Ng4 is an interesting option which deserves further exploration.) 13.Nf3 c6; 14.Be3 Nf7; 15.Rae1 Qd7. Here I think the strongest move is 16.Re2, yielding a flexible formation in which White has sufficient compensation for the pawn.

B2) **11...Bxg5!?** leads to 12.Bxg5 Nf7.

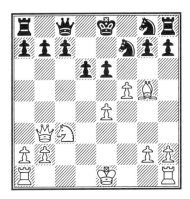

This defensive formation seems artificial and White maintains a strong initiative. (12...Nf6; 13.Bxf6 gxf6; 14.0-0 e5; 15.Nd5 Rf8; 16.Qh3 c6; 17.Qh5+ Kd7; 18.Qxh7+ Nf7; 19.Nxf6+ Kc7; 20.Qg7 Kb6; 21.Nh7. White won. Wise – Hoogendoorn, Hastings 1965) 13.fxe6! (13.Bh4?! exf5; 14.0-0 Ngh6; 15.exf5 0-0; 16.Nd5 Kh8; 17.Qc3 Qd7; 18.f6 g6; 19.Bg5 Ng4; 20.Qd2 Rae8 and Black was clearly better in Sogaard – Jadoul, 1988.) 13...Nxg5; 14.Qb5+ c6; 15.Qxg5 g6; 16.0-0 Qxe6; 17.Nd5! Black's position is precarious. Still, it is not clear that White has a way in after 17...Kd7!

B3) **11...exf5?!** is clearly inferior. 12.0-0.

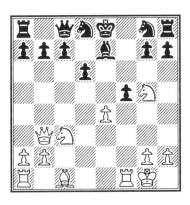

Black's king is trapped in the center and White is able to bring enough force to bear to break down the Black defenses. 12...h6 (12...Nh6; 13.Nd5 Bxg5; 14.Bxg5 Nhf7; 15.Bxd8 Qxd8; 16.Rxf5 Qd7; 17.Qxb7 0-0; 18.Raf1 Rac8; 19.Qxa7 h6; 20.Nb6 and White won in Klovan – Darzniek, Riga 1962.) 13.Nh3 Nf6; 14.exf5 c6; 15.Be3 Qd7; 16.Nf4 Qxf5; 17.Rae1 Qh7; 18.Bd4 Rc8; 19.Bxf6 gxf6; 20.Nfd5 also worked out victoriously for White in Liptay – Bokor, Budapest 1960.

GÖRING GAMBIT ACCEPTED
(Part Three)

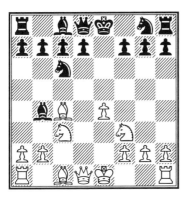

OPENING MOVES	
1.e4	e5
2.Nf3	Nc6
3.d4	exd4
4.c4	dxc3
5.Nxc3	Bb4

OVERVIEW

In this chapter, we present the main lines for Black in the **Göring Gambit Accepted**, as well as some remaining side lines.

In the diagrammed position, Black has a number of tries, and some come close to equalizing. Indeed this is one of the positions where Black can choose from many acceptable continuations and White must be prepared to meet each of them, while Black need only study one.

If that seems to be a practical limitation on the opening, you must also consider that most players are not prepared for the Göring Gambit at all, or perhaps just memorized a few plans from a book. Odds are, they've never defended against it before.

You, on the other hand, will have plenty of time to explore the White side of the opening. Experience is the best teacher!

GÖRING GAMBIT Accepted: Part Three	
6.Bc4 d6	
Options at move 6	58
Option 1: 6...Qf6	58
Option 2: 6...Bxc3+	59
Option 3: 6...Nge7	60
Option 4: 6...Nf6	61
7.0-0 Bxc3; 8.bxc3 Nf6	
Options at move 8	65
Option 1: 8...Bg4	65
Option 2: 8...Be6	67
Option 3: 8...Qe7?	71
9.e5 Nxe5; 10.Nxe5 dxe5; 11.Qb3 Qe7; 12.Ba3 c5; 13.Bb5+	
Options at move 13	76
Option 1: 13...Nd7?	76
Option 2: 13...Kf8	77
Option 3: 13...Bd7	80

6.Bc4! In this game, we examine the remaining reasonable alternatives to the main lines which begin with 6...Nf6, which we will examine at the end of this chapter.

6...d6. This is just one of Black's logical options. Black can add to the pressure at c3 by playing the queen to f6, can capture the knights with check, develop the knight at g8 to e7, or bring the knight to its normal home at f6.

Let's take a look at those plans.

GÖRING GAMBIT - OPTIONS AT MOVE 6

<u>1.e4 35; 2.Nf3 Nc6; 3.d4 exd4; 4.c4 dxc3; 5.Nxc3 Bb4; 6.Bc4 d6</u>
Option 1: 6...Qf6
Option 2: 6...Bxc3+
Option 3: 6...Nge7
Option 4: 6...Nf6

GÖRING GAMBIT, MOVE 6
Option 1: 6...Qf6

This is a premature development of the queen, who can quickly find herself exposed and vulnerable. 7.0-0 Bxc3; 8.bxc3 Ne5; (8...Nge7; 9.Bg5 Qg6; 10.Qd2 0-0; 11.Rfe1. White has the initiative, according to D. Smit.) 9.Nxe5 Qxe5; 10.Qb3 is a good plan for White.

10...Qe7! (10...Qh5 is artificial, and White can exploit this by advancing the e-pawn, gaining a permanent advantage in space to add to the power of the bishop pair. 11.e5 Ne7; 12.Ba3 b6; 13.Bxe7 Kxe7; 14.Qa3+ Kd8; 15.Rad1 Bb7; 16.Qa4 c6; 17.Ba6 Rb8; 18.Bxb7 Rxb7; 19.Qxc6 Rc7; 20.Qa8+ Rc8; 21.Qxa7 Qf5; 22.Rfe1 Qe6; 23.Rd6 Qe7; 24.Red1 Ke8; 25.Rxd7 Qe6; 26.Qb7. White won. Joksik – Zwetkovic, Postal 1987.) 11.Ba3 c5!; 12.Rad1 Nh6 (12...Nf6; 13.e5 Ng4; 14.h3 Nxe5; 15.Rfe1! and White is better, according to Ciocaltea.) 13.Rd5 b6; 14.f3 0-0. Black has castled, but the knight on h6 is out of play.

The White bishop at a3 does nothing now, but it has provoked the advance of the Black c-pawn. The bishop can now return to the kingside. 15.Rfd1 Kh8; 16.Bc1! Ng8; 17.Bf4!

White is clearly better here. The center is dominated and Black has no useful role for the bishop at c8. 17...Qd8; 18.Bd6 Re8; 19.R5d2. What can Black do about the pawn at f7, which is attacked twice but is undefended? 19...Re6 (19...f6; 20.Bf7 also wins the exchange.) 20.Bxe6 fxe6; 21.c4 Qf6; 22.a4 Bb7; 23.a5 Bc6; 24.axb6 axb6; 25.Qxb6 Ne7; 26.Qxc5 and White eventually won in Ciocaltea – Baretic, Vrsac 1971.

GÖRING GAMBIT, MOVE 6
Option 2: 6...Bxc3+

This is playable, of course, since Black usually captures at c3 sooner or later. For the most part, these lines will transpose into one of the main variations. Deviations from transpositional paths are not recommended. 7.bxc3.

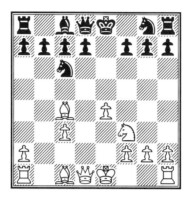

7...Nge7 (7...Nf6; 8.e5 Qe7; 9.0–0 Nxe5; 10.Nxe5 0–0; 11.Re1 d6; 12.Nxf7 Qd7; 13.Ne5+. White won. Ladee – Dragt, Postal 1975.) 8.Ng5 Ne5; 9.Bb3 h6; 10.f4 hxg5; 11.fxe5 Ng6; 12.0–0 Nxe5; 13.Bxf7+ Nxf7; 14.Rxf7 d5; 15.Rxg7 Qd6; 16.Qxd5 Qxh2+; 17.Kf2 Rf8+; 18.Ke3 g4; 19.Ba3. White won. Simunok – Philipp, Postal 1975.

GÖRING GAMBIT, MOVE 6
Option 3: 6...Nge7
The vulnerability of the pawn at f7 is now exposed.

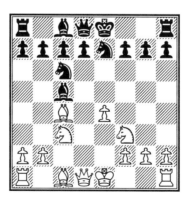

7.Ng5 Ne5; 8.Bb3 h6; 9.f4 hxg5; 10.fxe5 Bxc3+; 11.bxc3 is clearly better for White, with the bishop pair and targets at g5 and f7, Penrose – Soderborg, Budapest 1959.

GÖRING GAMBIT, MOVE 6
Option 4: 6...Nf6

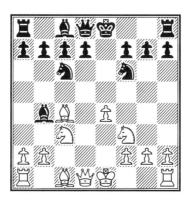

7.e5. White keeps the initiative by attacking the enemy knight. There are a lot of traps here, so Black must be very careful. Even if all the complications are evaluated correctly, White comes out with a decent game. **7...d5** is now essential.

A) 7...Ng4?? is an instructive error: 8.Bxf7+ Kxf7; 9.Ng5+ Kg8; 10.Qd5+. Black resigned, Casafus– Formanek, Lewisham 1981,

B) 7...Ne4?? also loses immediately: 8.Qd5 0-0; 9.Qxe4 and White went on to win in Amovilli – Schrammel, Postal 1988.

C) 7...Bxc3+; 8.bxc3 Ne4? just drops a piece to 9.Qd5.

8.exf6 dxc4; 9.Qxd8+.

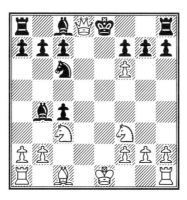

Now Black has a choice. Although it means giving up the right to castle, capturing with the king is better. **9...Kxd8!** After 9...Nxd8;

10.fxg7! it is hard to find a good plan for Black.

A) 10...Rg8; 11.Bh6 Bf5; 12.0-0-0 Bxc3; 13.bxc3 Ne6 (13...f6; 14.Rhe1+ Kf7; 15.Rd4 b5; 16.Rf4 Kg6; 17.Nh4+ Kxh6; 18.Nxf5+ Kg5; 19.Rf3. Black resigned. Grevlund – Binas, Postal 1980.) 14.Rhe1 Rd8; 15.Nd4 Rd5; 16.Nxf5 Rxf5; 17.f4 Rh5; 18.Bg5 Rxg5; 19.fxg5 Rxg7; 20.h4 and again Black was forced to capitulate, Richter – Claus, Postal 1975.

B) 10...Bxc3+; 11.bxc3 Rg8; 12.Bh6 Ne6; 13.0-0-0.

This position has been explored a few times but Black has not been able to find a solution to the problems of the king in the center. 13...Nxg7 is most easily met by giving check at e1. 14.Rhe1+! Be6!

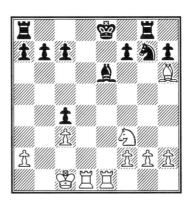

15.g4!? Rd8; 16.Nd4 Rd5; 17.f4 Rd8; 18.Bxg7 Rxg7; 19.Rxe6+! Black resigned, Gomilla–Burgues, Postal 1984.

So, Black captures with the king instead, and White replies by munching the g–pawn.

10.fxg7 Re8+! 10...Rg8 is too passive. 11.Bh6 Bxc3+; 12.bxc3 f6; 13.0–0–0+ Ke7; 14.Rhe1+ Kf7; 15.Re4 Be6; 16.g4 Rae8; 17.g5 f5; 18.Re2 Re7; 19.Rde1 Bd5; 20.Rxe7+ Nxe7; 21.Ne5+ Ke8; 22.g6 hxg6; 23.Nxg6. Black resigned. Pirrot – Gebhardt, Saarlouis 1986.

11.Be3 Bxc3+; 12.bxc3 Ke7! A clear, but nevertheless surprising plan. Black is simply going to capture the pawn at g7 with the king! 12...f6; 13.0–0–0+ Ke7; 14.Nd4 Nxd4; 15.Rxd4 Be6; 16.Rf4 gives White too much play, for example 16...Kf7; 17.Bd4 Kxg7; 18.Rxf6 Kg8; 19.Re1 Bg4; 20.Re5.

13.0–0–0 Kf6 14.Rhe1 Be6. This position was reached in Ljubojevic–Lombardy, Manila 1973. White can now try 15.Bh6 or 15.Nd4. The latter is more promising.

15.Nd4 Kxg7 16.Nxc6 bxc6.

Black's extra pawn is meaningless, and the tripled pawns are certainly a weakness. Still, once Black places the bishop at d5 and contests the open files, it will be very hard for White to win with bishops of opposite colors on the board. All in all, I'd keep on playing as White rather than accept a draw.

Returning to the Main Line

We will take **6...d6**, the most important alternative to 6...Nf6, as our main line, because this continuation is more complicated, even though 6...Nf6 has a better reputation in many circles.

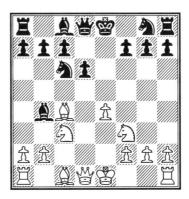

White now castles, not worrying about the structural damage that can be inflicted by capturing at c3.

7.0–0 Bxc3; 8.bxc3 Nf6.

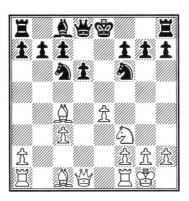

Black follows basic principles of sound development and does not create any glaring weaknesses, so we are going to have to play precisely if we want to get enough compensation for our pawn. We do have the bishop pair and a lead in development. On the other hand, our queenside is weak. Black has other playable plans. They are the development of the bishop to g4 or e6, and the aggressive stationing of the queen at e7.

GÖRING GAMBIT - OPTIONS AT MOVE 8

1.e4 e5; 2.Nf3 Nc6; 3.d4 exd4; 4.c4 dxc3;
5.Nxc3 Bb4; 6.Bc4 d6; 7.0-0 Bxc3; 8.bxc3 Nf6.
Option 1: 8...Bg4
Option 2: 8...Be6
Option 3: 8...Qe7?

GÖRING GAMBIT, MOVE 8
Option 1: 8...Bg4

Black wants to use the pin, but White can ignore the threat to the kingside.

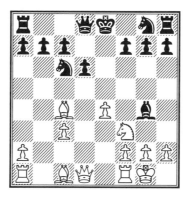

9.Qb3 Bxf3. White has time for an intermezzo before recapturing the bishop at f3.

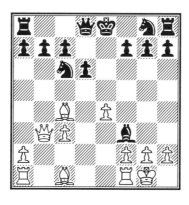

10.Bxf7+ Kf8; 11.gxf3! (11.Bxg8 Rxg8; 12.gxf3 allows Black too strong an attack on the kingside. 12...Qd7!; 13.f4 Qg4+; 14.Kh1 Qf3+; 15.Kg1 Re8; 16.Re1 g5; 17.Re3 gxf4+; 18.Qxg8+ Kxg8; 19.Rxf3 and White won Battes – Bisguier, New York 1991.) 11...Ne5; 12.Bxg8! Rxg8; (12...Nxf3+; 13.Kg2 Nh4+; 14.Kh1 Rxg8; 15.Rg1 Qf6; 16.f4 repels the Black attack.) 13.f4 Nf3+; 14.Kg2.

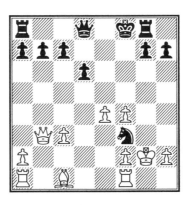

Black suffers from a weak kingside formation and the knight at f3 can easily become trapped. 14...Nh4+; 15.Kh1! Qd7; 16.f5!

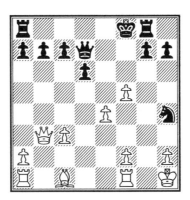

A) 16...Qc6! is correct, defending the pawn at b7 while attacking the one at e4. Black will add to the pressure with ...Re8, without allowing the pawn to fall as in the game. Surely this position is better for Black, so White must not enter into this line, despite the advice of Smith & Hall. 17.f3 (17.Qc2 Re8; 18.f3 also transposes below.) 17...Re8 reaches positions discussed below under 17.f3? but I don't see any alternatives for White.

B) 16...Re8? The analysts let this move pass without comment, but it is a critical error which should give Black the advantage. 17.Qxb7! This is an impressive move, introduced in the present game, but it is irrelevant now that we have seen that Black would have gained the upper hand with 16...Qc6!; 17...Qa4; 18.f3 Qc2; 19.Qb2 Qd3; 20.Qf2 g5; (20...h6 just weakens the kingside. 21.Bf4 g5; 22.fxg6 Nxg6; 23.Bxh6+ led to a White win in Ammers – Van Der Kooij, Postal 1982.) 21.Bxg5.

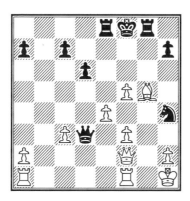

This invites a pretty finish. 21...Rxe4!; 22.Bxh4 Re2; 23.Qxa7! Rgg2 Black is lost anyway. 24.Qb8+ Kg7; 25.f6+ Black resigned, since checkmate is inevitable. Milukas – Stutkus, Vilnius 1966.

GÖRING GAMBIT, MOVE 8
Option 2: 8...Be6
White now weakens Black's position by exchanging bishops.

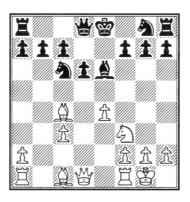

9.Bxe6 fxe6; 10.Qb3. The typical pawn structure of the lines where Black opposes a bishop at c4 with a bishop at e6 has been reached.

As usual, Black has a choice of defending the pawn at b7 or sacrificing it for an open line and an initiative. The sacrificial line offers more chances for Black to obtain equality.

A) 10...Qc8; 11.Ng5 Nd8 (11...Ke7?; 12.f4 b6; 13.f5 Na5; 14.Qd1 e5; 15.Qd5 Nh6; 16.Ne6 c6; 17.Bg5+ Kd7 lets White finish brilliantly.

18.Qxd6+!! and in Rev – Jankovic, Pristina 1974, Black resigned in view of 18...Kxd6; 19.Rd1#.) 12.f4 h6; 13.Nh3 Qd7; 14.Ba3. White has a lot of pressure here, well worth the investment of the pawn. 14...Qc6; 15.Kh1 Ne7; 16.Rae1 0-0; 17.f5 a5; 18.Nf4 a4; 19.Qd1 e5; 20.Nh5 Nc8; 21.Bc1 Rf7; 22.Qg4 Kh8; 23.f6 g5; 24.Ng7 Qxc3; 25.Qh5 Rxf6; 26.Bxg5 Rxf1+; 27.Rxf1 Kg8; 28.Qg6 and White won in Ribli – Kovacs, Budapest 1970

B) 10...Qd7!; 11.Qxb7 Rb8; 12.Qa6.

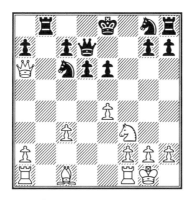

Here 12...Nge7 is an interesting move. Smith & Hall claim that their new move 13.Be3 brings White an advantage, but I do not agree. We must therefore consider some other options for White.

13.Be3 (13.Bg5 0-0; 14.Rfd1 Ng6; 15.Qa4 allows 15...Rxf3; 16.gxf3 Rf8 and Black has plenty of compensation for the exchange. For example 17.Be3 e5!; 18.Kf1 Nh4. Bjerring – Lein, Varna 1974. Black has plenty of compensation for the exchange, since a pawn is coming at f3 and the queen can quickly join the rook and the knight in an attack on the White king. So perhaps White should choose 13.Ng5 0-0; 14.Be3 h6; 15.Nf3. The tempting 15...Rxf3 may be premature: 16.gxf3 Rf8; 17.Qe2 Ne5; 18.f4 N5g6; 19.Qg4.)

13...0-0; 14.Ne1.

Smith & Hall claim an advantage for White on the grounds that the knight will operate effectively from d3 and the bishop on e3 is powerful. But this assumes that the center will remain static. Black can test White's plan immediately by advancing the pawn to d5, and then has a threat of fxe4. To meet this, White will likely respond with f3. A logical move for Black is 14...d5.

15.f3 invites (15.exd5 Nxd5; 16.Bc5 Rf5 is more than a little awkward for White. The c-pawn is hanging. 17.Rd1 Qe8; 18.Rd3 Nf4; 19.Rf3 Rxc5; 20.Rxf4 Rxc3 and Black is clearly better.) 15...Rb2; 16.Nd3 Rc2! A small annoyance which forces White's hand. 17.Rfc1 Rxc1+; 18.Rxc1 Qe8! (18...dxe4 is not yet available because of 19.Nc5!) 19.Nc5 (19.Bxa7 dxe4; 20.Nb4 exf3; 21.Nxc6 Nxc6 is better for Black. The attack on White's king will make it difficult for White to provide resources to defend the weak queenside pawns.) 19...Qg6; 20.Kh1 Rb8 and Black has play on both sides of the board.

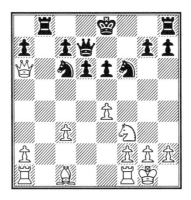

The standard advance of the e-pawn does not seem to work here. 13.e5 Nd5; 14.exd6 cxd6; 15.Ba3 Nxc3! White must do something to establish an initiative before Black castles. 16.Bxd6!? Qxd6; 17.Rac1 0-0; 18.Rxc3 Rb6!; 19.Qe2 Nd4; 20.Nxd4 Qxd4. Black should draw without difficulty, and did. 21.Rc4 Qf6; 22.Rfc1 Rb2; 23.R4c2 Rxc2; 24.Qxc2 Qd4; 25.Qe2 Kh8, Tsharotshkin – Juergen, Postal 1992.

GÖRING GAMBIT, MOVE 8
Option 3: 8...Qe7?

This recklessness is simply inviting disaster.

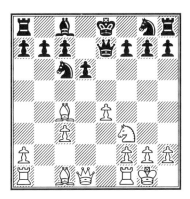

9.Ba3 Ne5; 10.Nxe5 Qxe5; 11.f4! Qxc3 (11...Qe7 runs into 12.e5.) 12.Bb5+ Bd7; 13.Rf3 Qa5; 14.Bxd7+ Kxd7; 15.Rb3 Nh6; 16.e5 d5; 17.Rxb7 Rab8; 18.Bb4 Black resigned, Van Der Tol – Hart, Postal 1990.

Returning to the Main Line

So we settle on **8...Nf6.**

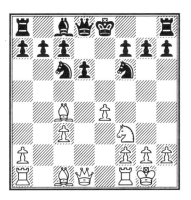

9.e5.

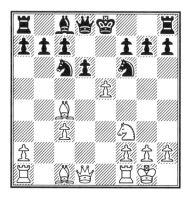

This is White's most aggressive option.

9...Nxe5. Capturing with the knight is Black's best chance, and now we encounter the area where White must really work hard even to maintain equality.

9...dxe5?!; 10.Ng5! This looks like a beginner's move, but f7 is actually weak here. Obviously bad is 10...Qxd1? because of 11.Bxf7+ Kf8; 12.Rxd1 and Black is busted.

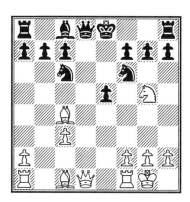

One reasonable move is 10...Be6 to which White should reply 11.Nxe6! fxe6; 12.Qb3 Na5 (12...Nd5; 13.Qxb7 Na5; 14.Bb5+ c6; 15.Bxc6+ Nxc6; 16.Qxc6+ Kf7; 17.Rd1! looks dangerous for Black. 12...0-0; 13.Bxe6+ Kh8; 14.Ba3 Re8; 15.Rad1 Qb8; 16.Bd7 Nxd7; 17.Rxd7 gives Black problems on both sides of the board.) 13.Qb5+ c6; 14.Qxe5 Nxc4; 15.Qxe6+ Qe7; 16.Qxc4 0-0-0 (16...Nd5; 17.a4 followed by Ba3.) 17.Qa4 is a piece of analysis from Rolf Schwarz.

White certainly has compensation for a pawn, and Black has no counterplay. So, Black should perhaps attend to king safety with 10...0–0. Here we play 11.Ba3 and White is raking the diagonals.

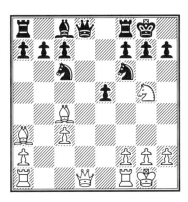

We can easily see that 11...Bg4 gets clobbered: 12.Qb3! Na5 (12...Bh5; 13.Bxf8 Qxf8; 14.Qxb7 Na5; 15.Qxc7 and the attack on the knight at a5 prevents ...Rc8.) 13.Bxf7+ Kh8; 14.Qa4 hitting the knight at a5 and the rook at f8.

This leaves the plan of exchanging queens. 11...Qxd1; 12.Raxd1 Bf5?! (12...Bg4 is better. 13.f3 Bh5; 14.Bxf8 Kxf8; 15.Rb1. Smith & Hall break off here, claiming White is on top. Perhaps, but an improvement must be found on 15...h6!; 16.Ne4 Nxe4; 17.fxe4 Na5; 18.Bd3 Rd8; 19.Bc2 Be2; 20.Rf2 Bc4; 21.Rd1 Rxd1+; 22.Bxd1 b6; 23.Rd2 Ke7; 24.Kf2 Nb7; 25.Ke3 Nc5; 26.g3 a5; 27.h4 f6 which was agreed drawn in Michalek – Uhmann, Karvina 1989.) 13.Bxf8 Rxf8; 14.Rfe1 h6; 15.Nf3.

This square would not have been available had Black chosen 12...Bg4 instead of 12...Bf5. 15...Bg4; 16.Rb1 e4; 17.Nd4 Ne5; 18.Bf1.

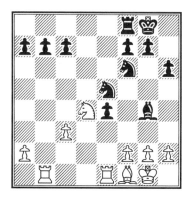

White is retreating, and Black has a material advantage. Appearances can be deceiving, however. 18...c5; 19.Nb5 c4; 20.f3! This exploits the pin on the pawn at e4. Of course it does permit Tal to make a small sacrifice, but Yukhtman had calculated well. 20...Bxf3; 21.gxf3 Nxf3+; 22.Kf2 Ng4+; 23.Kg3 Nxe1; 24.Rxe1 f5; 25.Bxc4+ Kh7.

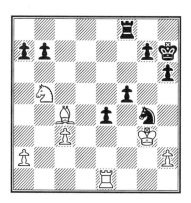

This position was surely evaluated by both players back at move 20. White has an extra piece, but Black has three pawns as compensation and White's remaining pawns are weak. The bishop is strong, however, and Yukhtman's confidence was justified. 26.Be2! Ne5; 27.Kf4 Ng6+; 28.Ke3. The king is used to blockade the pawns. Tal desperately tries to create some counterplay. 28...f4+; 29.Kd4 Kh8; 30.Rg1 Nh4; 31.Kxe4 Re8+; 32.Kd3 f3; 33.Bd1 Ng2; 34.Kd2. White's pieces are just close enough to stop the f-pawn. 34...Nh4; 35.Nd4 Rd8; 36.Rf1 Rd5; 37.Kd3 Ra5; 38.Bb3.

White has everything under control, and Black can resign at any time. 38...g5; 39.Nxf3 Rf5; 40.Nd2. White won. Yukhtman – Tal, Soviet Championship 1959.

Returning to the Main Line

So we must return to Black's plan of capturing the pawn with the knight. **9...Nxe5; 10.Nxe5 dxe5.**

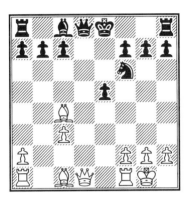

Although more pieces have left the board, White retains good compensation. **11.Qb3 Qe7.** 11...0–0; 12.Ba3 wins the exchange, since the rook must stay home to guard f7. **12.Ba3 c5; 13.Bb5+.**

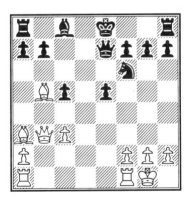

Now Black has to decide between interpolating the bishop and sliding the king to f8. So, how does Black respond to the check? Even though we are already at move 13, there is plenty of practical experience to guide us. We'll consider three moves.

Interposing the bishop is the normal move, and it seems to give Black the better game. 13...Kf8!? forfeits the right to castle, but threatens to explode on the queenside with ..a6, ...b5 etc. White has been unable to demonstrate a path to full compensation for the pawns, so it is a very important path. Less significant is the knight block, which loses a pawn.

GÖRING GAMBIT - OPTIONS AT MOVE 13

1.e4 35; 2.Nf3 Nc6; 3.d4 exd4; 4.c4 dxc3;
5.Nxc3 Bb4; 6.Bc4d6; 7.0-0 Bxc3; 8.bxc3 Nf6; 9.e5 Nxe5;
10.Nxe5 dxe5; 11.Qb3 Qe7; 12.Ba3 c5; 13.Bb5+.
Option 1: 13...Nd7
Option 2: 13...Kh8
Option 3: 13...Bd7

GÖRING GAMBIT, MOVE 13
Option 1: 13...Nd7?

A mistake, which allows White to cash in on the light squares.

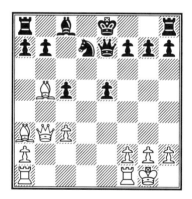

14.Bxd7+ Bxd7; 15.Qxb7 0-0; 16.Rad1 gives White sufficient pressure for the pawn. 16...Rfd8; 17.Rd2 Qe8; 18.Bxc5 Bc6; 19.Rxd8 Rxd8; 20.Qc7 Rc8; 21.Qxa7 Ra8; 22.Qc7 Rxa2; 23.Rd1 Ba4; 24.Re1 f6; 25.h3 h6; 26.Rb1 Qc6; 27.Qa7 Qe4; 28.Rb4 Qd5; 29.Rb7. White won. Velimirovic – Littleton, 1966.

GÖRING GAMBIT, MOVE 13
Option 2: 13...Kf8

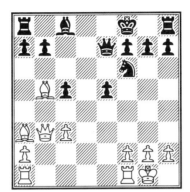

The best you can do here is to play **14.f4** and try to open up the position. For example:
A) 14...Be6!?

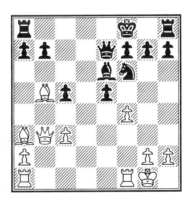

15.c4 (15.Qa4 is White's best, according to Smith & Hall, but I see absolutely nothing for White after 15...Nd5; 16.f5. This was the move they relied on. 16...Nb6!; 17.Qg4 Bd7 and I don't see White holding enough compensation for two pawns, though the position remains complicated.) 15...exf4; 16.Rxf4 h5; 17.Qe3 Rc8; 18.Re1 Rh6; 19.Rf5 b6; 20.Bb2 Rg6? (20...Rd8!? is good, unless White can sacrifice the queen. 21.Qxh6 gxh6; 22.Rxf6 Rd2 and now 23.Rexe6 Qxe6; 24.Rxe6 fxe6; 25.Be5 Rxa2 leaves White with no way of stopping the inevitable advance of the queenside pawns.) 21.Rg5 Rxg5; 22.Qxg5 Qd6; 23.Rf1 Rd8; 24.h3 Qd2; 25.Qe5 Qd6 was agreed drawn in

Niedermaier – Van Perlo, Postal 1975.
  B) 14...e4; 15.f5. We are still two pawns down and what do we
have to show for it? Not a lot. Yet there are some encouraging factors.

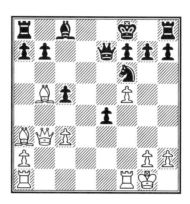

  Again Black has several choices, and White should be familiar
with each of them. None of them are at all bad.
  B1) Black can get off the dangerous diagonal with 15...Kg8.
Now on 16.Rad1 b6; 17.Bc6 Bb7; 18.Bxb7 Qxb7; 19.Bxc5. White wins
back one of the pawns, but at the cost of simplification. 19...h6; 20.Bd4
Re8; (20...Kh7; 21.Bxf6 gxf6; 22.Qb4 Rae8; 23.Rf4 e3; 24.Qd4 is better for White, according to analysis by Nikitin.) 21.Bxf6 gxf6 and the
annoying pawn at e4 keeps the White rooks away from the kingside.
  The Black king will be safe at h7. Still, the Black pawns are weak,
and I think that after 22.Rfe1! White has chances to either win the
pawn at e4 or swing the rook to the h-file with an attack.
  B2) 15...b6!? The fianchetto can be played immediately, or in
conjunction with other moves. 16.Rad1 Bb7; 17.Bc1 e3; 18.Be2 h5;
19.Rd3 Qe4; 20.Rf3 Ng4; 21.Rg3 Re8; 22.f6 gxf6; 23.Bxe3 Nxe3;
24.Rdxe3 Qxe3+; 25.Rxe3 Rxe3; 26.Kf2 Re7; 27.Qd1 Kg7; 28.Bxh5
Be4; 29.h3 Rhe8; 30.c4 Re5; 31.Bf3 Bxf3; 32.Qxf3 Re4; 33.Qg3+ Kh7;
34.Qc7 R8e7; 35.Qd6 R7e6 was agreed drawn Widenius – Korhonen,
Postal 1990.
  B3) **15...h5!** is the most worrisome move. Black is finding a
way to get the rook at h8 into the game. **16.Rad1 Qc7; 17.Bc4 Ng4!;
18.g3 Ne5.**

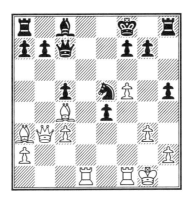

Now Black is the one with the attack. 19.f6 Bh3!; 20.Rd5 (20.fxg7+ Kxg7 and the Black king is still safe.) 20...b6; 21.Rxe5. A desperate attempt to strike at the Black king. 21...Qxe5; 22.fxg7+ Kxg7; 23.Rxf7+ Kg6; 24.Bc1 b5! The point is to set up ...Be6. 25.Qa3 a6; 26.Kf2 Rh7. White resigned.

So we don't have a convincing refutation of Black's plan. This is not at all unusual in gambit play. After all, if there were no way for Black to get a decent game, they'd never allow the opening to be played! With 14...Be6, the line ends in a draw. 14...e4 is more lively, or deathly, but here too the gambiteer never gives up hope.

Going back to that last line, let's consider **19.Bd5**, attacking the e-pawn, instead of letting Black's bishop enter the game. Sure Black can play **19...Nf3+,** but then we can sacrifice the exchange with **20.Rxf3!? exf3; 21.Bxf3.** In return for the material, a rook and pawn for a bishop), we get to keep the pressure on and Black has to find a way for the rooks to get into the game. Note that the f-pawn cannot be captured.

21...Bxf5?; 22.Rd5! g6; 23.Rxc5 really piles on the pressure. Black can try 21...Rh6, but even so 22.Rd5 gives some counterplay. Now **23...Qb6** pins the rook, but after **24.Bxb7 Rb8; 25.Qxb6 axb6; 26.Rc7+ Kg7; 27.Bd5** White has enough compensation.

So, we get to the interpolation of the bishop, which is the normal continuation.

GÖRING GAMBIT, MOVE 13

Option 3: 13...Bd7

White should now exchange bishops.

14.Bxd7+ Qxd7.

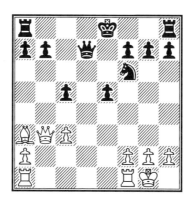

14...Nxd7 is summarily dismissed by Smith & Hall on the basis of the capture at b7, but an actual game showed that Black is not without resources. 15.Qxb7 Rb8!; 16.Qxa7 0-0; 17.Rfd1 and Black has the saving trick 17...Ra8!; 18.Qxd7 (18.Rxd7! Rxa7; 19.Rxe7 Rxe7; 20.Bxc5 Rc7; 21.Bxf8 Kxf8; 22.Rc1 and Black will have to suffer a bit.) 18...Qxd7; 19.Rxd7 Rxa3; 20.Rd5 Rxc3. Drawn. Chudinovsky – Sakharov, Soviet Championship 1979.

15.Bc5.

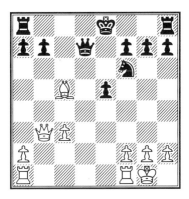

Black has two lines here. Repositioning the queen at c6 with tempo is logical, but the more aggressive leap of the knight to e4 is risky. **15...Qc6.** 15...Ne4; 16.Ba3 (16.Qa3 Qc6 transposes to the main line with 15...Qc6.) 16...Nd2 (16...0-0-0 deserves consideration, for example 17.Qc4+ Qc6; 18.Qxf7 Kb8; 19.c4 Qf6; 20.Qxf6 gxf6; 21.Rfe1 Rd4; 22.f3 Nd6; 23.Bxd6+ Rxd6; 24.f4 was agreed drawn in Sprinkhuizen – Stoll, Postal 1989.) 17.Qb4 0-0-0! (17...Nxf1? is much too greedy and is swiftly punished. 18.Rd1 Qe6; 19.Qb5+ Qc6; 20.Qxe5+ Qe6; 21.Qxg7. White won. Ribli – Imre, Hungary 1968.)

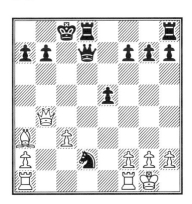

18.Rfd1 Qc7; 19.c4 Ne4; 20.c5 Nf6; 21.Rd6 Rd7; 22.Rad1 Rhd8 23.Qe1 is good for White, e.g., 23...Re8; 24.Rb1 Re6; 25.Bb4 Rexd6 26.cxd6 Qb6; 27.Rc1+ Kb8; 28.Bc5 Qb2; 29.Bxa7+ Kxa7; 30.Qa5+ Kb8; 31.Rc8+ Kxc8; 32.Qa8# Holthuis – Van Oirschot, Postal 1987.

16.Qa3 Ne4.

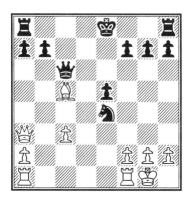

Here White has enough for the pawn, but Black should be able to hold a draw.

17.Be3 Nd6. 17...Qxc3; 18.Qa4+ Qc6; 19.Qa3 with a draw is Ribli's conclusion. **18.Rab1 0–0; 19.Bc5 Rfd8; 20.Rfe1 Nf5; 21.f3 b6; 22.Bf2 f6; 23.Red1 Qc7; 24.Qb3+ Qf7; 25.Kf1 Rac8; 26.Rxd8+ Rxd8; 27.Ke2 g5; 28.a4 Qxb3; 29.Rxb3 Rd7** was peacefully concluded in Klop – Laarhoven, Postal 1975.

GÖRING GAMBIT DECLINED

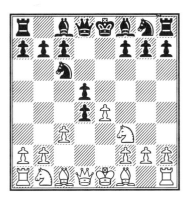

OPENING MOVES

1.e4	e5
2.Nf3	Nc6
3.d4	exd4
4.c3	d5

OVERVIEW

It is unfortunate that one is no longer obliged to accept gambits and sacrifices, as that quaint custom from the past led to many magnificent battles. Declining gambits often leads to sterile and less interesting positions. As Black, it is far more uncomfortable to suffer the attacks which inevitably arise in gambit play, than to calmly decline the offer and get on with a normal life.

The plan with an early ...d5 is the most popular method of declining the gambit. In the **Göring Gambit Declined**, Black avoids most of the risks associated with the opening, and with correct play, has only a small positional disadvantage in the main lines. White normally captures at d5 and accepts an isolated d-pawn. The nature of the struggle is quite different from the Göring Gambit Accepted, but White still has the initiative and a promising attacking formation.

This is the most annoying continuation from White's point of view. If you don't want to settle for sterile equality, you may need to make an investment of a pawn or two. Be well prepared, however, and you will have the edge in preparation and experience to rely on!

GÖRING GAMBIT
Declined

5.exd5 Qxd5; 6.cxd4

Options at move 6	84
Option 1: 6...Nf6	84
Option 2: 6...Bg4	86

5.exd5 Qxd5; 6.cxd4 and Black can either develop or pin the knight at f3.

GÖRING GAMBIT - OPTIONS AT MOVE 6

1.e4 e5; 2.Nf3 Nc6; 3.d4 exd4; 4.c3 d5; 5.exd5 Qxd5; 6.cxd4
Option 1: 6...Nf6
Option 2: 6...Bg4

GÖRING GAMBIT DECLINED, MOVE 6
Option 1: 6...Nf6

Once again the development of the knight to f6 is a normal response, if not as ambitious as 6...Bg4.

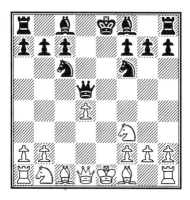

It comes down to a question of which side Black wants to castle on. Opposite wing castling is riskier but can bring greater rewards. This does not mean that winning chances are more abundant, however. The calmer approach can be effective if Black possesses better endgame technique.

Great players like Anatoly Karpov can win many of the "drawn" endgames. Studying endgames may be, for some, a better use of time than preparing intricate and lengthy variations in the sharper lines.

7.Be2 Bf5.

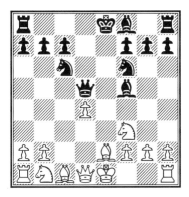

This is Wolf's patent. Black has alternatives. 7...Bg4 tranposes to the 6...Bg4 lines. (7...Bb4+; 8.Bd2 8.Nc3 transposes to Velimirovic – Tringov. 8...Qd6; 9.0–0 0–0; 10.Be3 Nd5; 11.a3 Ba5; 12.Nbd2 Nxe3; 13.fxe3 Qh6; 14.Nc4 Bb6; 15.Qd3 Re8; 16.Rae1 f6; 17.Bd1 Kh8; 18.Ba4 Bd7; 19.Nxb6 axb6; 20.Bxc6 bxc6; 21.e4 was a little better for White in Gershov – Margolin, Moscow Championship 1995.)

8.Nc3 Bb4; 9.0–0.

A) 9...Qa5 is playable here. Black delays the capture until White plays a3.

B) 9...Qa5; 10.Bd2 (10.Bb5 Bxc3; 11.Bxc6+ bxc6; 12.bxc3 is nothing special for White.) 10...0–0; 11.a3 Bxc3; 12.bxc3 Ne4; 13.Qc1 Nxd2; 14.Nxd2 (14.Qxd2 Rfe8 should also be equal.) 14...Rfe8; 15.Bf3 Qa4; 16.Qb2 b6; 17.Rfe1 Rad8; 18.Be2 a6; 19.Nf1 b5; 20.Ng3 Qc2; 21.Qc1

C) 9...Bxc3; 10.bxc3 0–0.

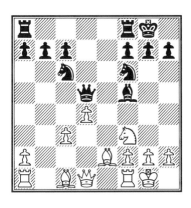

This is another fairly typical position. The bishop at f5 keeps White from putting a rook on the b-file. 11.c4!? The advance of the central pawns is risky, because it makes the pawns vulnerable to counterattacks, but it also gains a spatial advantage in the center. 11...Qe4 12.d5 Nb4; 13.Nd4 Rfe8. Marco notes that although Black has five pieces in play, compared with White's two, he has to trade off active pieces soon. 14.Be3 Nc2.

This is logical, since the White knight is more effective than its Black counterpart. 15.Nxc2 Qxc2; 16.Bf3! Qxd1 (16...Qxc4 can get clobbered, as Marco shows: 17.Rc1 Qxa2; 18.Rxc7 Rab8; 19.d6 Qa6; 20.d7 Red8; 21.Bxb7!! Rxb7; 22.Rc8 Qa5 and now the elegant 23.Qa4!! works.) 17.Rfxd1.

White has the advantage in this endgame, thanks to the bishop pair. If Black can exchange the b-pawn and c-pawn for White's c-pawn and d-pawn, a draw is likely provided that the a-pawn does not fall. 17...Bg4 Black decides to eliminate the light-squared bishops. But now White will be able to get to b1. Mieses – Wolf, Carlsbad 1907.

GÖRING GAMBIT DECLINED, MOVE 6
Option 2: 6...Bg4
The pin is easily broken with **7.Be2.**

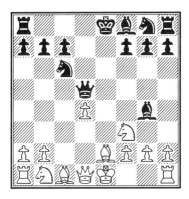

The position resembles a Scandinavian Defense, except that White's c-pawn and Black's e-pawn have been removed. This works to Black's advantage, as it is easier to develop the kingside pieces. One major factor for White, however, is that the c-file can be used to attack the Black king if castling takes place on the queenside.

7...Nf6.

A) 7...Bxf3 is premature. 8.Bxf3 Qc4 prevents White from castling immediately, but that is all that it accomplishes. 9.Be3 also looks good. 9...Bb4+; 10.Nd2 Nxd4; 11.Bxd4 Qxd4; 12.Qe2+ Kf8; 13.0-0-0 Re8; 14.Ne4 Qe5; 15.Qc4 a5; 16.Rd7 Ne7; 17.Rhd1 Qf4+; 18.Kb1 Nc6; 19.Qd5 Be7; 20.Nc5 Nb4; 21.Qe4 Qf6; 22.Rd8 Black resigned, Luijk – Vosselman, Bergen 1977.

B) 7...0-0-0 puts more pressure on the pawn at d4.

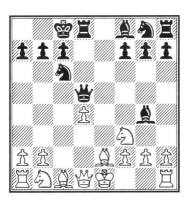

This is the most exciting line, but Black is taking major risks. The queenside seems quiet, for the moment, but White can build a queenside attack very quickly. 8.Be3 is a good but perhaps unappreciated resource. White will defend d4 and then castle queenside, since Nc3 comes with tempo. 8...Nh6; 9.Nc3 Qh5; 10.Qa4 Nf5; 11.d5 Nxe3; 12.fxe3 Bxf3; (12...Nb4 is no better. 13.e4 Bc5; 14.a3 Bd7; 15.Qb3 Na6; 16.Bxa6 bxa6; 17.Qc4 and White is better.) 13.Bxf3 Qe5; 14.0–0-0!

White gives up the e-pawn, but gets his king to safety so that a big queenside attack can be launched. 14...Qxe3+; 15.Kb1 Nb4?! Black is too concerned with the a-pawn, or perhaps missed the following variation. (15...Ne5!?; 16.Rhe1 Qg5; 17.Qxa7 Nxf3; 18.gxf3 Qg6+!; 19.Ka1 Qa6; 20.Qxa6 bxa6 and Black is no worse.) 16.d6 Bxd6; 17.Rxd6 Rxd6; 18.Qxb4 Rb6; 19.Qg4+ Kb8; 20.Qxg7 and White is clearly better.

8.Nc3.

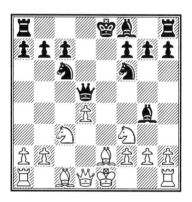

Black now must do something about the queen.

8...Qa5. This is the main line, but alternatives must be considered.

A) 8...Qd8; 9.0-0 Be7; 10.h3 Bf5; 11.d5 Nb8; 12.Nd4 Bc8; 13.Bb5+ Bd7; 14.Nf5 0-0; 15.Bxd7 Qxd7; 16.Qf3 Bb4; 17.Nxg7 Kxg7; 18.Bh6+ Kg6; 19.Qf4 Qf5; 20.Qxb4 was much better for White, since the bishop at h6 cannot be captured as the rook at f8 is hanging, Dubinsky – Moldavsky, Soviet Teams1964.

B) 8...Qh5; 9.h3 Bd6!; 10.Be3!? 0-0?! (10...0-0-0!? deserves consideration.) 11.Qb3 Nb4; 12.0-0-0 Be6; 13.Qa4 Bd7; 14.Qb3 Qa5; 15.Ne5 is complicated.

C) 8...Qf5; 9.0-0 Bd6; 10.h3 Bxf3; 11.Bxf3 is better for White.

D) 8...Bb4; 9.0-0 with three ways of removing the heat from the queen.

D1) 9...Qa5?; 10.Bd2! Qf5 (10...Bxc3; 11.bxc3 0-0 would be similar to the 9...Bxc3 lines, but with the queen committed to a5.) 11.d5! Nxd5; 12.Nd4 Nxd4; 13.Bxg4 Qd3; 14.Nxd5. White won. Frilik – Dullmann, West Germany 1976.

D2) 9...Qd6; 10.Nb5 Qe7; 11.d5 0-0-0; 12.Bg5 a6; 13.Nbd4 Rxd5; 14.Nxc6 bxc6; 15.Bxf6 gxf6; 16.Bxa6+ Kd7; 17.Ne5+ fxe5; 18.Qxg4+ Ke8; 19.Bb7 and White was better in Horvath – Mestrovic, Keszthely 1981.

D3) 9...Bxc3! This is probably the only playable line. 10.bxc3 0-0. White has the bishop pair and greater control of the center. 11.h3 Bf5; (11...Bh5; 12.Bf4 Qd7; 13.Rb1 is better for White.) 12.c4 and White has an initiative.

9.0-0 0-0-0.
9...Bd6; 10.h3 Bd7 (10...Bh5; 11.Qb3 0-0-0; 12.Be3 and the battle will be decided on one of the flanks. White's king looks safer to me.) 11.Nb5 0-0; 12.Nxd6 cxd6 was equal in Pribik – Paroulek, Postal 1984. 13.Bf4

10.Be3.

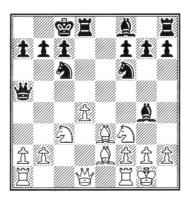

Any gambit player should enjoy the attacking possibilities on the queenside. Black usually tries to establish the knight at d5 in order to stop the d-pawn from advancing and threatens to exchange itself for one of White's potential attacking pieces.

10...Nd5. Black has tried many plans here, and White must be prepared to adapt as needed.

A) 10...h5; 11.a3 Nd5; 12.Nxd5 Qxd5; 13.b4 h4; 14.h3 Be6; 15.Qd2 f6; 16.b5 and White had a strong initiative in Pirrot – Kargoll, West Germany 1985.

B) 10...Bc5; 11.a3! Bxf3 (11...Bb6; 12.Nb5 Bxf3; 13.gxf3 Nxd4; 14.Nxd4 wins for White, Penrose – Prames, Munich (Olympaid) 1958.) 12.b4 Bxe2; 13.Qxe2 Bxb4; 14.axb4 Qxb4; 15.Nb5 gives White a strong attack.

C) 10...Nb4; 11.Ne5 Be6; 12.a3 Nbd5; 13.Nb5 Nxe3? Black should retreat the queen to b6 and keep the knight at d5 as a blockader. 14.fxe3 Kb8; 15.b4 gives White a tremendous queenside attack, Prada – Coleby, Postal 1987.

D) 10...Bd6 is met by 11.h3! and now Black had better exchange on f3, with an admittedly inferior position. 11...h5?! is too optimistic. 12.Nb5 Qb6; 13.d5 Bc5; 14.Bxc5 Qxc5 and White gets the upper hand with 15.Rc1! Qxd5; 16.Qa4 Qe6.

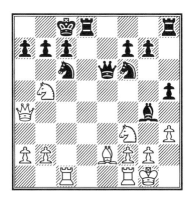

Now the typical sacrifice finishes things off. 17.Rxc6 bxc6; 18.Nxa7+ Kd7; 19.Nxc6 Bxf3; 20.Bxf3 Ra8; 21.Rd1+ Nd5; 22.Rxd5+ Qxd5; 23.Na7+. White won. Stoker – Samson, Postal 1971.

E) 10...h6 is slow: 11.a3 Nd5 (11...Be7; 12.b4 Qf5; 13.b5 Bxf3; 14.Bxf3 Ne5; 15.Be2 looks promising for White.) 12.Nxd5 Qxd5; 13.b4 is analysis from Botterill (1986) who notes that the attack on the queenside will continue with Qa4. White stands better.

F) 10...Be6; 11.a3 Nd5; 12.Bd2 leaves Black in search of a reply, Levy – Pritchett, Glasgow 1969.

11.Nxd5 Qxd5.

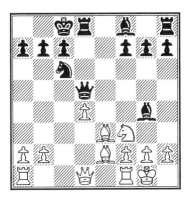

This is the normal continuation. **12.Rc1!? Bd6; 13.Qa4 Rhe8.**

This is a very common type of position. White now breaks through with a temporary exchange sacrifice.

14.Rxc6! Qxc6; 15.Bb5 Qd5. 15...Qe4!? deserves attention. 16.Ng5 Qe7; 17.Bxe8 Qxe8; 18.Qxa7 may be met by 18...f6! **16.Bxe8 Bxf3; 17.gxf3 Qxf3.**

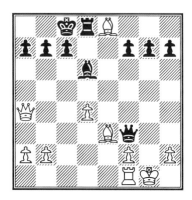

White's bishops are not very active, but Black is down a piece. **18.Re1 Qh3; 19.f4 Qg4+.** The hunt begins, but is quickly abandoned. **20.Kf2 Qh4+; 21.Ke2 Qe7; 22.Bb5.** White went on to win in Germlin – Janes, Soviet Team Championship 1976.

Summary

That's a lot of material on the Göring Gambit! You don't need to memorize it all, just observe the patterns and the key positions and you will get comfortable with it, and hopefully make your opponent uncomfortable at the same time!

Now we move on to the mighty and complicated Sicilian Defense, but there we will adopt a plan that is so rare that it can be absorbed very quickly.

SICILIAN DEFENSE
• Halasz Gambit •

OPENING MOVES	
1.e4	c5
2.d4	cxd4
3.f4	

OVERVIEW

The **Halasz Gambit** is quite different from the better known Smith-Morra Gambit, where White offers the c-pawn immediately. I don't think it is better than the Smith-Morra, but the theory of that opening has grown so complex that it cannot be handled properly in a book of this scope. It is a different matter with the Göring Gambit, which has less diversity in the defenses, but to play the Smith-Morra, you need to study a tremendous amount of theory. After that heavy experience in the Göring, we choose some more restricted territory for our Sicilian adventures.

The more obscure Halasz Gambit will come as more of a surprise to your opponents. At first, they may not recognize how the advance of the f-pawn leads to positions which hold secrets of their own. To begin with, Black finds it more difficult to hold on to the pawn.

A key element in White's strategy is control of the f5-square. White is content to let the Black pawn at d4 remain on the board. Since it is not easily sup-

SICILIAN DEFENSE HALASZ GAMBIT	
3...Nc6	
Option at move 3	94
Option 3...d6	94
4.Nf3 Qb6	
Option at move 4	98
Option 1: 4...g6	98
Option 2: 4...d5	99

ported by a colleague at e5, the pawn can be regained by force after Nf3. Nevertheless, there are times when White chooses to gambit the pawn with a later c3. This does not lead to a Smith-Morra Gambit because in that opening the f-pawn usually remains at f2, blocked by a knight at f3. Your opponent is not likely to be familiar with this opening, and that will provide a psychological advantage.

One thing to keep in mind is that although Halasz, the player, racked up a tremendous score as White, his opposition was very weak and in many cases he obtained just enough cooperation from his opponent to salvage a bad position. I have tried to introduce improvements for White which give a more realistic chance of obtaining full compensation for the pawn.

Therefore, I recommend using the Halasz Gambit in conjunction with normal f4 Sicilians, keeping your opponents off guard. White can often transpose into main line Sicilians where f4 is a useful move. Sicilian players are aware of that, of course, and will often adopt a formation which is part of their normal repertoire.

Here Black may automatically respond 2...Nc6. Of course if your opponent usually plays the popular Najdorf Sicilian, then 2...Nc6 is not such a good choice, as after 3.Nf3 and 4.Nxd4, play can transpose into a Classical Sicilian, a line that a Najdorf player may not know. So there are useful transpositional tricks that you can use from the Halasz Gambit. Najdorf and Dragon players will likely play 3...d6, a line we'll look at below.

The Main Line
With **3...Nc6** Black sensibly defends the pawn at d4. That's the main line, but we must carefully consider the alternative.

HALASZ GAMBIT - OPTION AT MOVE 3
Option 1: 3...d6

HALASZ GAMBIT, MOVE 3
Option 1: 3...d6
This is the normal choice of the Dragon or Najdorf player. It keeps open both transpositional options and allows Black to play ...e5 to try to hold the pawn at d4.
4.Nf3

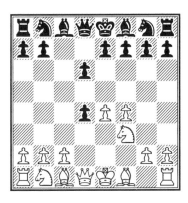

A) **4...Bg4** is designed to discourage recovery of the pawn. 5.Bd3 (5.Qxd4 Bxf3; 6.gxf3 Nc6 is fine for Black.) 5...Nc6; 6.0–0 Nf6 is Halasz – Grossmann, Postal 1988. Now White chose 7.a3, which makes no sense to me since ...Nb4 is in no way a threat. Instead, I suggest 7.h3 Bxf3; 8.Qxf3 e6; (8...e5; 9.Bc4 gives White more than enough compensation for the pawn. Black's kingside is not well supported.) 9.Nd2 Be7; 10.e5 with a complicated position that holds good chances for White. For example, 10...Nd5; 11.Nc4 Rc8; 12.exd6 Bxd6; 13.f5 with a strong attack.

B) **4...Nf6** creates pressure on the center. It is too soon to advance the e-pawn, so it must be protected. **5.Bd3 Nc6; 6.0–0.**

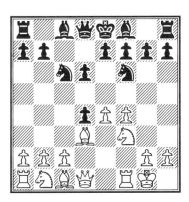

6...e5 (6...Bg4; 7.h3 Bxf3; 8.Qxf3 e5 seems logical but after 9.g4! White has a strong kingside attack, for example 9...Be7; 10.a3 a5; 11.f5 h6; 12.Nd2 d5; 13.Kg2 dxe4; 14.Nxe4 Nxe4; 15.Bxe4 Rc8; 16.Bd2 0–0; 17.f6 Bxf6; 18.Qf5, Halasz – Muller, Postal 1988.)

7.h3. This move is played to prepare the advance of the g-pawn and keep enemy pieces off of g4.

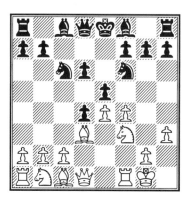

B1) 7...Be7 8.c3?! is an overly ambitious attempt on Halasz's part. (8.Nbd2 0-0; 9.Nc4 is much more promising.) 8...dxc3; 9.Nxc3 0-0; 10.Qe2 (10.Be3 exf4; 11.Bxf4 Qb6+; 12.Rf2 allows 12...d5!; 13.Nxd5 Nxd5; 14.exd5 Bc5 and Black is clearly better.) 10...Nh5; 11.Rd1 Nxf4; 12.Bxf4 exf4; 13.Nd5 Bf6; 14.Nxf4 Qb6+; 15.Kh1 Qxb2 gave Black too much material in Halasz – Engel, Postal 1980.

B2) 7...a6 8.Qe1. The queen often operates from g3 or h4 during the kingside attack. 8...Be7; 9.a3? Halasz often plays this move, but I find it irrelevant. Why not an immediate g4, especially since the Black knight can't even get to b4 because the White queen covers that square. (9.g4 Qc7; 10.Qg3 0-0; 11.c3 dxc3; 12.Nxc3 gives White the same sort of counterplay found in the Smith – Morra Gambit. White will play Be3 or Bd2, Rac1, and continue with the kingside attack. The rook can later move from c1 to c2 for transfer to the g – or h -file.) 9...0-0; 10.g4 exf4; 11.Bxf4 Nd7; 12.Nbd2 Nde5; 13.Qg3 was played in Halasz – Rau, Postal 1984. 13...Nxd3; 14.cxd3 g5! would have won on the spot for Black.

Returning to the Main Line
3...Nc6. Black sensibly defends the pawn at d4.

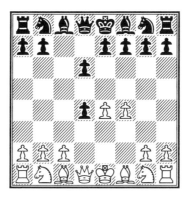

4.Nf3 Qb6. This is the move that holds the pawn. Most others allow transpositions to normal Sicilians after Nxd4, though that is not our intention in this repertoire.

4...d6; 5.Bd3 e5; 6.0–0 Nf6; 7.h3 transposes to the 3...d6 lines, below.

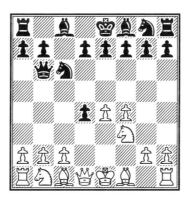

We must consider two other logical moves. Black can fianchetto the bishop on the kingside, or try the Sicilian break at d5 immediately.

HALASZ GAMBIT - OPTIONS AT MOVE 4
1.e4 e5; 2. d4 xcd4; 3. f4 Nc6; 4. Nf3 Qb6
Option 1: 4...g6
Option 2: 4...d5

HALASZ GAMBIT, MOVE 4
Option 1: 4...g6

The fianchetto is not without risk, since the White f-pawn is ready to undermine the pawn structure and open a route to h6 for the bishop by advancing.

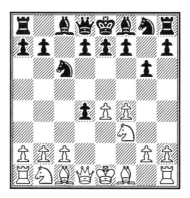

5.Bd3 Bg7; 6.0-0 Nf6; 7.Qe1 is good for White, since the enemy kingside is easy to attack with Qh4 and f4. Black can react with the "Sicilian break", placing a pawn at d5 to disrupt the center.

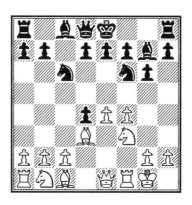

7...d5!?; 8.e5 Ne4; 9.Nbd2 Nxd2; 10.Bxd2 Qb6. Black plays aggressively. Castling comes into consideration, though White already has enough compensation for the pawn. 11.b4 (11.Qg3!? may be an effective gambit. 11...Qxb2; 12.Rfb1 Qa3; 13.Rb3 Qc5; 14.Rb5 Qa3 and here White can of course draw by repetition with Rb3, but more interesting, if riskier, is 15.Rxd5 0-0; 16.Rb5 with an unclear position.) 11...a6 (11...Bf5; 12.a4 Bxd3; 13.cxd3 gives White enough compensation, as the pawn at d4 is weak and can be recovered if necessary.) 12.a4 Bg4; 13.b5 Bxf3; 14.a5!

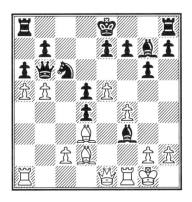

This intermezzo swings the game in White's favor. 14...Qc7; 15.bxc6! Be4; 16.cxb7 Qxb7; 17.Rb1 White has the initiative now and will not give it up! 17...Qc7; 18.Bxe4 dxe4; 19.Qxe4 0-0; 20.Rb7 and White won quickly in Halasz – Johansen, Postal 1983.

HALASZ GAMBIT, MOVE 4
Option 2: 4...d5
The advance of the d-pawn to d5 is usually the equalizer in the Sicilian, and it is a good move here.

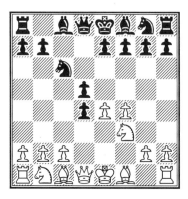

5.e5 (5.exd5 Qxd5; 6.Nc3 Qe6+; 7.Ne2 looks strange, but Black's pieces are so awkwardly placed that it may be playable. 7...Nf6; 8.Nfxd4 Nxd4; 9.Qxd4 should be about equal.) 5...Qb6; 6.Bd3 Nh6. This odd looking move makes sense here because the knight is headed for f5. 7.a3.

White needs to expand on the queenside and play Bb2 to regain the pawn. The kingside does not offer anything at the moment. 7...Bf5; 8.0–0 e6; 9.b4 Rc8; 10.Nbd2 (10.Bb2 Ng4; 11.Bxf5 d3+; 12.Kh1 Ne3 and Black is much better,) 10...Bxd3; 11.cxd3 Nf5; 12.Nb3 is Halasz – Niemand, Postal 1984. Here Black incomprehensibly sacrificed a piece at b4 and went down in flames. After the more sensible 12...Be7; 13.Qe2 0–0; 14.Bb2 a5! White has nothing better than 15.Nxa5 Nxa5; 16.bxa5 Qxa5; 17.Rfc1 and Black's extra pawn is not worth much, but it is not going away.

So, we return to the position after **4...Qb6,** where White will reply **5.Bd3.**

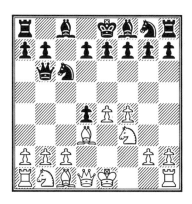

With this move White declares that the recovery of the pawn is not a high priority. The emphasis here is on development and castling as soon as possible.

5...d6. 5...Nf6; 6.0-0 d5; 7.e5 Ne4; 8.Nbd2 (8.Qe2 is a worthwhile alternative.) 8...Nc5; 9.Nb3 Nxd3; 10.cxd3 Bf5; 11.Nh4 Bd7; 12.Qe2 e6; 13.f5 Nb4; 14.fxe6 Bxe6; 15.Nf5 was played in Halasz – Nilsson, Postal 1976.

6.0-0 g6; 7.Nbd2 Bg7; 8.a3.

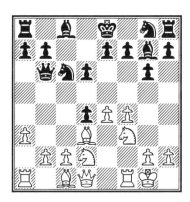

The point of this move is not to keep enemy pieces from b4, but rather to occupy that square with a pawn and control queenside space.
8...Nf6; 9.h3 e5; 10.b4 a6; 11.g4. Now that the queenside is resolved, the kingside attack begins in earnest.

11...0-0; 12.Qe1 Qc7; 13.f5 h6? 13...d5! is the best defense. 14.Qg3 dxe4; 15.Nxe4 Nd5 and here after 16.fxg6 hxg6; 17.g5 the position is messy. One possibility is 17...Nce7; 18.Nf6+ Nxf6; 19.gxf6 Bxf6; 20.Bh6 Rd8; 21.Rae1 Nf5; 22.Bxf5 Bxf5; 23.Nxe5 and if Black captures at c2, then White can build pressure on the kingside. 23...Qxc2; 24.Ng4 Bxg4; 25.hxg4 Bh8; 26.Re7.

Of course matters are by no means clear. 26...d3; 27.Qf3 Bd4+; 28.Kh1 Qc6 gets the queens off. 29.Qxc6 bxc6; 30.Rfxf7 and White is still fighting for a draw.

14.fxg6 fxg6; 15.Bc4+ Kh8; 16.Nh4 Ne7; 17.Qe2 b5; 18.Bd3 Be6; 19.Ndf3 Nd7; 20.Bd2 Nb6; 21.g5 h5.

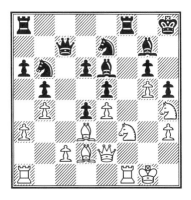

Now it is clear that White is not going to get anywhere without a sacrifice but which one? A knight can be offered at d4, g6, or f5. **22.Nf5!?** Is this really sound. It isn't clear. As a practical matter, the defense is difficult. **22...gxf5; 23.g6! fxe4; 24.Ng5.** Now we see the power of White's attack. The threat of Qxh5+ and Qh7 mate looms. **24...Bg4; 25.hxg4**

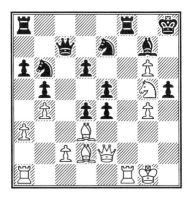

25...Qd7. 25...exd3; 26.Qh2 Ng8; 27.Nf7+! and White wins. On the other hand, 25...Rxf1+; 26.Rxf1 Nxg6; 27.Bxe4 forks rook and knight. **26.Bxe4 Qxg4+; 27.Qxg4 hxg4; 28.Bxa8 Rxa8.**

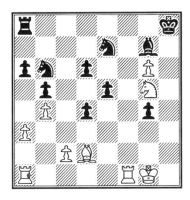

We have entered a very unusual endgame. Black has a knight and two pawns for the rook, and will win the pawn at g6. The Black pawns are very weak, however. More importantly, the bishop at g7 has very limited mobility. All of White's pieces now converge on the kingside. **29.Rf7 Nxg6; 30.Ne6! Bf8; 31.Rf6 Nh4.** If 31...Kh7, then 32.Kf2! and the rook at a1 will have a lot to say!

32.Nxf8. White has an extra rook and the three pawns are not enough compensation. **32...Nf3+; 33.Kg2 Kg7; 34.Rxd6 Nc4; 35.Bh6+** and Black resigned in Halasz – Gaida, Postal 1985. This is the most impressive example of the Halasz Gambit. As our analysis shows, White cannot always get enough tangible compensation for the pawn, but there are many attacking chances and it is very easy for the defender to slip up.

FRENCH DEFENSE
• Alapin Gambit •

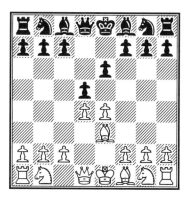

OVERVIEW

The **Alapin Gambit** is a favorite of Blackmar–Diemer Gambit (1.d4 d5; 2.e4) fans and can lead to similar positions on the board. In other words, the gambit does not quite work, but Black must play with exceptional care.

Reverend Tim Sawyer, author of the best study on this obscure line, points out that in his database White won 72 of the games, and Black won a mere 18, with just a 10% draw rate. Of course the overwhelming majority of these games are played by amateurs, which means that their defensive skills were not up to the task of handling the protection of their king.

Black does not have to accept the gambit, but this is the best course of action and the true test of the soundness of the opening.

I will concentrate here on what I consider to be the best defense, and refer anyone interested in the opening to Sawyer's wonderful *Alapin French*.

This is a real fun gambit, so enjoy it!

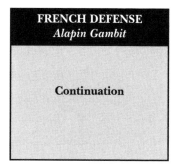

FRENCH DEFENSE
Alapin Gambit

Continuation

3...dxe4; 4.Nd2 Nf6; 5.f3. This is the thematic move, but there are alternatives, such as 5.c3 or 5.c4. They are a bit slow, however. **5...exf3**.5...Nd5; 6.Qe2 exf3; 7.Ngxf3 is another form of defense, and it is also good. Black must not play slowly, however.

For example, 7...b6 (Sawyer evaluates 7...Bd6; 8.0–0–0 0–0; 9.Ne4 Bf4; 10.Bxf4 Nxf4; 11.Qd2 Ng6; 12.h4 Qd5; 13.Nc3 Qh5; 14.Be2 as equal. I doubt that White has quite enough for the pawn, but there is certainly room for a kingside attack.) 8.Qf2 c5; 9.Ne5 f6; 10.Bb5+ Nd7; 11.0–0 Nxe3; 12.Nc6. This is a complicated position, but White is much better and went on to win in Rasa – Foord, Postal 1961.

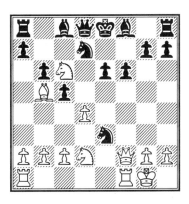

What Black missed was the forcing variation, not played in the game, that would lead to a hopeless endgame: 12...Nxf1; 13.Nxd8 Nxd2; 14.Nxe6 Ne4; 15.Qf3 Bb7; 16.Nc7+ Kd8; 17.Nxa8 Bxa8; 18.Re1 and Black's material compensation of three pieces for the queen falls to pieces, e.g., 18...a6; 19.Bxd7 Kxd7; 20.Rxe4 Bxe4; 21.Qxe4 and the pawns start dropping.

6.Ngxf3 Be7; 7.Bd3 b6; 8.0–0 Bb7; 9.Bg5.

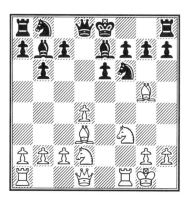

Rev. Sawyer has played both sides of this position. He comments that Black will find it difficult to reach the endgames, which are likely to be favorable if not too many compromises are made during the defensive stage of the middlegame.

9...0-0. 9...Nbd7; 10.Qe1 c5. Recommended by Sawyer in his book, but without mentioning this game. 11.Bb5 Sawyer proposes 11.dxc5, 11.c3 and 11.Qh4. I doubt that any of them come close to equality, but White's move in the game is pointless once Black castles. 11...0-0; 12.Bd3 cxd4; 13.Qh4 g6; 14.Nc4 Nd5; 15.Nd6 Rb8; 16.Nxd4 Bxg5; 17.Nxf7 Be3+; 18.Kh1 Qxh4. White resigned, Black – Sawyer, USA 1988.

10.Qe1.

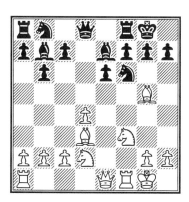

10...Nc6. Sawyer labels this as a mistake, yet look at what happens after the alternatives!

10...Nbd7; 11.Qh4 Re8; 12.Bxf6 Nxf6; 13.Ng5 Qd5; 14.Bxh7+

Kf8; 15.Be4 Qxd4+; 16.Kh1 Bxe4; 17.Qh8+ and Black resigned before getting suffocated by Nxe6 mate in Sawyer – Lindy, Hatboro 1989.

10...c5; 11.Qh4 h6. This is an invitation to disaster, and the reverend delivers a storm of biblical proportions. (11...g6; 12.Rae1 Nc6 and it is hard to see a convincing continuation for White.) 12.Bxh6 gxh6; 13.Qxh6 Qd5; 14.g4.

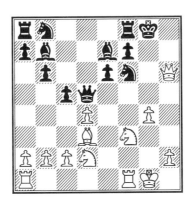

14...c4 (14...cxd4; 15.g5 Nbd7; 16.gxf6 Nxf6; 17.Kh1 Qh5; 18.Rg1+ Qg6; 19.Bxg6 Bxf3+; 20.Nxf3 fxg6; 21.Qxg6+ Kh8; 22.Qg7# Sawyer – Katz, Postal 1991/92.)15.Nxc4 Nbd7; 16.Ne3 Qc6 would have put up more resistance. Of course, White could now bail with the perpetual check, but perhaps there is something else to try?

17.g5 Ne4; 18.g6 fxg6; 19.Qxg6+ Kh8; 20.Qh6+ Kg8; 21.Rf2 gets the rook to the g-file, since the knight is pinned to the h7 square. 21...Bf6 (21...Rxf3; 22.Rxf3 Ng5; 23.Rg3 Qh1+; 24.Kf2 Rf8+; 25.Nf5!!) 22.Rg2+ Kf7; 23.Ne5+ Bxe5; 24.dxe5 Ke7; 25.Qh4+ Ke8 and now the quiet 26.Be2 keeps the pressure on, with two pawns and an attack for the piece. On the other hand, Black has possibilities on the kingside.

11.c3 Ne8; 12.Qh4 h6; 13.Ne4.

A standard Blackmar – Diemer method of attack. All of the pieces are in useful positions except for the rook at a1. Nevertheless, Black's position is defensible.

13...Bxg5; 14.Nexg5 Nf6; 15.Rae1 Re8. 15...Ne7 is much stronger, and there may be nothing better than entering the endgame after 16.Ne4 Nxe4; 17.Bxe4 Bxe4; 18.Qxe4 Qd5; 19.Qxd5 Nxd5 and Black has an extra pawn for nothing tangible.

16.Ne5 Nxe5; 17.Rxe5 hxg5; 18.Rxg5 Kf8; 19.Rxg7 Kxg7; 20.Qg5+ Kf8; 21.Rxf6 Qd5; 22.Rxf7+ Kxf7; 23.Bg6+ Kg7; 24.Bf5+ Kf7; 25.Bg6+.

So White managed to draw, despite being two rooks down, in Sawyer – Snapstys, Hatboro 1989!

CARO-KANN DEFENSE
• Ulysses Gambit •

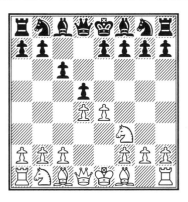

OPENING MOVES

1.e4   c6
2.d4   d5
3.Nf3

OVERVIEW

The offer of the pawn at e4 is a very unusual strategy in the Caro-Kann and it is almost certain to take your opponents by surprise. In the **Ulysses Gambit**, you will sacrifice the e-pawn, at least temporarily, and in some cases may offer up the d-pawn too.

It is likely that your opponent will return the pawn quickly, as I did as Black in the game cited below. In this case, you should be content with your advantage in space and recoup your material. Then you have a fairly normal Caro-Kann, but not one which you will find in the books because of the unusual move order applied.

The ultimate target of our attacks will be our old friend at f7, that vulnerable point that so often captures the attention of a gambiteer. You'll combine the knight at g5 with the bishop at c4 to put pressure on the weak square.

The Caro-Kann is usually the choice of players who don't mind defending. Often they count on winning various endgame positions which can be quite complicated. That's the thinking from the Black side. White's going to attack and make Black's life unpleasant. That's our thinking.

CARO-KANN DEFENSE *Ulysses Gambit*	
3...dxe4; 4.Ng5 Nf6; 5.Bc4 e6; 6.Nc3 Bb4	
Options at Move 6	*111*
Option 1: 6...Be7	111
Option 2: 6...b5!?	112
Option 3: 6...Nbd7	113

109

3...dxe4; 4.Ng5.

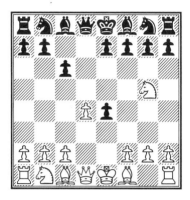

The Ulysses Gambit is quite interesting, even though it is largely neglected by theoreticians. The idea is similar to one which is now the main line of the Karpov Variation (1.e4 c6; 2.d4 d5; 3.Nc3 dxe4; 4.Nxe4 Nd7; 5.Ng5) except that here it is the knight at g1 that gets to g5. The gambit is a specialty of Clyde Nakamura of Hawaii.

4...Nf6. 4...Bf5 is a sensible alternative. White can try 5.c3!? (5.f3 Nf6; 6.Nc3 exf3; 7.Nxf3 leaves White a tempo down on a Blackmar – Diemer Gambit.) 5...h6 (5...e6; 6.Qb3 Qd7; 7.Nd2 Nf6; 8.Nc4! gives White good compensation, as the White knight threatens to get to e5 and double up on the pawn at f7. 8...Bg6; 9.Bf4 Be7; 10.Ne5 Qc8; 11.0–0–0 Nd5!; 12.Nh3 is unclear, but a gambiteer should be satisfied with the situation.) 6.Nxf7! Kxf7; 7.Qb3+ e6; 8.Qxb7+ Nd7; 9.Qxc6 gives White enough compensation for the piece.

5.Bc4 e6; 6.Nc3.

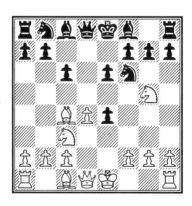

White will now regain the pawn at e4, and for the moment the bishop at c8 is locked in. **6...Bb4.** This is the strongest test of the gambit. Black parts with the bishop pair but hangs on to the pawn for a while.

We'll explore a few diversions here. The bishop can develop simply at e7, a common enough reply. Adventures on the queenside with the advance of the b-pawn can be risky, but can bring great rewards. Supporting the knight at f6 with its colleague at d7 is a solid plan.

ULYSSES GAMBIT - OPTIONS AT MOVE 6

<u>1.e4 c6; 2.d4 d5; 3.Nf3 dxe4; 4.Ng5; Nf6; 5.Bc4 e6; 6.Nc3 Bb4</u>
Option 1: 6 ... Be7
Option 2: 6 ... b5
Option 3: 6 ... Nbd7

ULYSSES GAMBIT, MOVE 6
Option 1: 6...Be7
Both sides hasten to complete development.

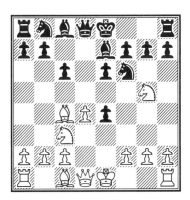

7.0–0 0–0. Now the capture. 8.Ncxe4 Nxe4; 9.Nxe4 was better for White in Nakamura – Perry, Hawaii 1986.

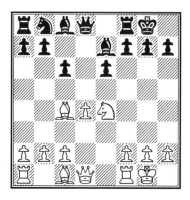

Black has a bad bishop which is not likely to enter the game anytime soon. White obtains a similar advantage in our primary game.

ULYSSES GAMBIT, MOVE 6
Option 2: 6...b5!?

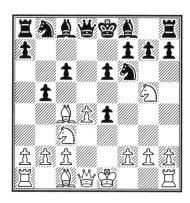

This surprising move is perhaps playable. The plan is reminiscent of the Semi-Slav, but the queenside formation is quite different here, with the pawn back at c2 and the e-pawn gone from the board. Of course this involves a positional concession in that the pawn structure is weak and the bishop at c8 remains very bad, but perhaps Black can take the initiative.

For example 7.Be2 Bb4!; 8.0–0 Bxc3; 9.bxc3 h6; 10.Nh3 0–0 where Black holds on to the pawn, though White has some compensation in the bishop pair and Black suffers from a miserable bishop at c8, which might be activated by an early ...e5.

So I recommend trying 7.Bb3, for example 7...a5; 8.a4! Bb4; 9.0-0! Even after 9...Bxc3; 8.bxc3 h6; 9.Nh3.

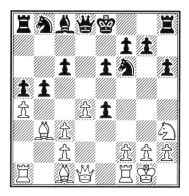

White has the advantage. The bishop pair and active position more than makes up for the pawn, which remains weak. Black must castle before Ba3 is played, but even so, the dark squares will remain weak.

ULYSSES GAMBIT, MOVE 6
Option 3: 6...Nbd7
This move is played with the intention of swapping knights at e4 and then bringing the knight from d7 to f6.

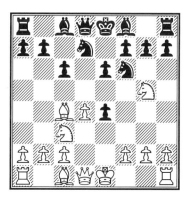

7.0-0 h6 (7...Bd6; 8.Re1 Qc7; 9.h3 0-0; 10.Ngxe4 is a level position, but the bishop at d6 must relocate and the Black kingside does not have much in the way of defense. There is still the problem of the Bc8 for Black to deal with.) 8.Ngxe4 Nxe4; 9.Nxe4 Nf6; 10.Qd3! The queen can take an active role in the game, as it is safe from enemy attacks. 10...Be7; 11.Be3 Qc7; 12.Rad1.

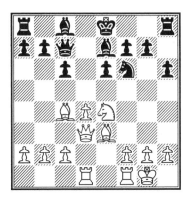

White certainly stands better here, with equal material, better development, and considerable pleasure from the awful bishop at c8. I decided to get the bishop into the game by fianchettoing it at b7 and playing an early ...c5. 12...b6; 13.f3 Bb7; 14.Rfe1 Rd8. There is no rush to play ...c5 right away, since Black has not finished developing. 15.Bf2 0-0; 16.Bg3 Qd7; 17.h3 c5.

A) 18.dxc5 Qxd3; 19.Bxd3 (19.Rxd3 Nxe4; 20.fxe4 Rxd3; 21.Bxd3 Bxc5+ gives Black the better endgame.) 19...Nxe4; 20.Bxe4 Rxd1; 21.Rxd1 Bxe4; 22.fxe4 Bxc5+; 23.Bf2 Bxf2+; 24.Kxf2 Rc8; 25.c3 Rc7 should be drawn, eventually.

B) 18.c3 is an option. 18...cxd4; 19.cxd4 Bd5; 20.b3! Bc6; (20...Bxc4; 21.bxc4 gives White control of the center.) 21.a4 Nd5; 22.Nf2? White overlooks the threats on the dark squares. 22...Bb4! White had nothing better than to give up the exchange with 23.Ng4 Bxe1; 24.Bxe1 but after 24...Nf4!; 25.Qe3 Ng6. Black consolidated and eventually won in Nakamura – Schiller, Hawaii International 1995.

So, we return to the main line, **6...Bb4,** where the bishop moves to b4 right away and pins the knight.

7.0–0 Bxc3; 8.bxc3 h6; 9.Nh3.

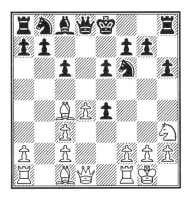

The Black pawn at e4 is no longer under attack. If ...e5 can be played quickly, then White will have a hard time justifying the investment of the pawn. Nevertheless, Black's task is not so easy.

9...Qa5.

9...Nbd7; 10.Bb3 e5; 11.dxe5 Nxe5; 12.Qxd8+ Kxd8; 13.Bf4 gives Black the opportunity to earn cuteness points with 13...Nf3+; 14.gxf3 Bxh3 but after 15.Rfd1+ Kc8; 16.fxe4 Nxe4; 17.Re1. White will pick up the pawn at f7 and the bishop pair will provide a small advantage.

10.Qe1 0–0; 11.f3 c5; 12.fxe4 Nxe4. 12...cxd4; 13.e5 Nd5; 14.cxd4 Qa4; 15.Qg3! Qxc4?; 16.Bxh6 Qxd4+; 17.Kh1 g6; 18.Bxf8 and White is up on the exchange, since 18...Kxf8??; 19.Qxg6 Nf4; 20.Qh6+ Ke8; 21.Qh8+ Ke7; 22.Rad1 wins.

13.Qxe4 Qxc3; 14.Bxh6!

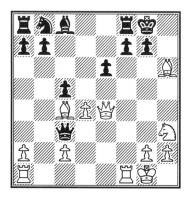

14...gxh6; 15.dxc5 Nc6; 16.Rae1 Rd8; 17.Rxf7 Kxf7; 18.Qh7+ Ke8; 19.Qg8+ Kd7; 20.Qf7+ Ne7; 21.Rd1+.

Riskier is **21.Qxe6+ Kc7; 22.Qxe7+ Rd7; 23.Qe4 Qd4+; 24.Nf2 Qxc5; (24...Qxe4; 25.Nxe4** gives White more than enough compensation for the exchange.) **25.Be6 Rd6; 26.Qh7+ Kb8; 27.Bxc8 Qxc8; 28.Qf7!** and there is enough play for the pawn.

Now **21...Kc7; 22.Qxe7+ Rd7; 23.Rxd7+ Bxd7; 24.Qd6+ Kd8; 25.Qf8+ Kc7; 26.Qd6+** draws.

PIRC DEFENSE
Short Attack (Part One)

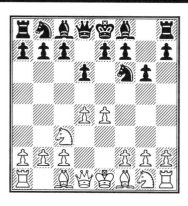

OVERVIEW

The Pirc Defense is not as popular as it has been in the past. Often Black delays deploying the knight at f6, and sometimes doesn't even bother with a fianchetto (see the chapter on the Czech Defense for 3...c6). Nevertheless, when White plays Bc4, Black often chooses to play an early ...Nf6, so we will see this line via transposition (from 1.e4 g6; 2.d4 Bg7; 3.Nc3 d6; 4.Bc4 Nf6).

One of the advantages of the **Short Attack** is that you can almost always get your knight to c3 and bishop to c4, so it is hard for Black to avoid. England's Nigel Short is not the first player to use this attack, but he is the player responsible for bringing it to the attention of top level tournament players.

The key components are a rapid deployment of the bishop at c4 and the stationing of the queen at e2. White then has sufficient support for the advance of the e-pawn.

Black can easily get crushed like a bug in this system.

PIRC DEFENSE *Short Attack: Part One*	
4.Bc4 Bg7; 5.Qe2 Nc6; 6.e5 Nxd4; 7.exf6 Nxe2; 8.fxg7 Rg8; 9.Ngxe2 Rxg7	
Options at move 9	*119*
Option 1: 9...c6	119
Option 2: 9...Bf5	121
Option 3: 9...c5	122
Option 4: 9...e5	122
10.Bh6 Rg8; 11.0-0-0 Be6	
Options at move 11	123
Option 1: 11...e6	124
Option 2: 11...c6	124
Option 3: 11...e5	125
Option 4: 11...Bf5	126

4.Bc4 Bg7. This move is more or less automatic and Black gains nothing by delaying it. If Black tries 4...a6, then don't worry about ...b5. It is especially important to avoid moves like a4 that open up the b4 square for Black. Just play 5.Qe2 and stick with the plan. 5...b5 6.Bb3 b4 is nothing to worry about because you can just play 7.Qc4, since 7...bxc3 loses to 8.Qxf7+ Kd7; 9.Be6+ Kc6; 10.Bd5+.

5.Qe2. With this move we trade control of the d4-square for more pressure on the efile. In addition, we prepare to castle queenside. **5...Nc6.** This is the move that takes up the challenge., All alternatives are quite passive, and the advance of the e-pawn proves annoying, for example 5...c6; 6.e5 dxe5; 7.dxe5 Nd5; 8.Bd2 Be6; 9.0–0–0 Nd7; 10.f4 N7b6; 11.Bb3 a5; 12.a3 and White had a promising kingside attack in Galloway – D.Gurevich, USA 1985. **6.e5.**

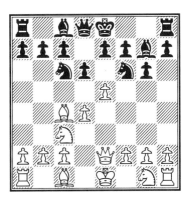

Here is our gambit. Although it has no generally recognized name, we'll credit Nigel Short for bringing it to the attention of professionals, and he did so when he was quite young. The Short Attack is well named for another reason. We will give up the pawn at d4 forcing massive complications, which turn out quite well for White. The game can be short indeed!

6...Nxd4. There is a lot of ground to cover in this system, so we will devote three entire chapters to it. In this section we will look at the acceptance of the gambit, though that is not really the most popular continuation. Declining with 6...Ng4, the main line, is in the next chapter and then we will look at a few odds and ends in the chapter after that.

7.exf6. The next few moves are forced. **7...Nxe2; 8.fxg7 Rg8; 9.Ngxe2.**

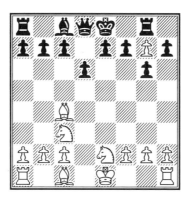

9...Rxg7.

Black should grab the pawn while it is still undefended. Nevertheless, Black has often tried to delay the recapture. Other options include battling for the d5-square with 9...c6, developing the bishop at f5, expanding on the queenside with 9...c5 or planting a stake in the center with 9...e5.

SHORT ATTACT: PART ONE - OPTIONS AT MOVE 9
Option 1: 9...c6
Option 2: 9...Bf5
Option 3: 9...c5
Option 4: 9...e5

SHORT ATTACK: PART ONE, MOVE 9
Option 1: 9...c6

Black hopes to get in ...e5 and ...d5 with a powerful pawn center.

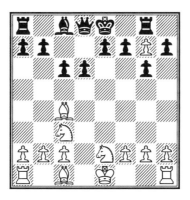

10.Bh6 hold on to the pawn and gives Black some problems in development..

A) 10...e6; 11.h4 d5; 12.0-0-0 Qe7; 13.Nf4 Bd7; 14.Bxd5 0-0-0; 15.Bb3 Be8; 16.g3 Rxd1+; 17.Rxd1 Bd7; 18.Ne4 f6; 19.Rxd7 Kxd7; 20.Bxe6+ Qxe6; 21.Nc5+ and Black resigned in Chandler – White, Edinburgh 1980.

B) 10...Qa5.

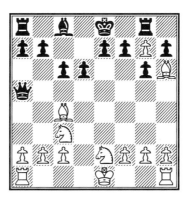

This is not well known, but it looks like Black's best plan. 11.0-0-0 b5; 12.Bb3 b4; 13.Ne4 and now:

B1) 13...Be6 looks like the strongest move. The obvious capture 14.Bxe6 may not be best. (14.Nd4 Bxb3; 15.Nxb3 comes into consideration. Instead of going for the a-pawn, which leaves the queen offside, Black should stick to the plan of dislodging the bishop from h6. 15...Qh5; 16.Bd2 c5; 17.Rhe1! 0-0-0; 18.Ng5 Rd7; 19.Nxf7 Rxg7; 20.Ng5 Qxh2; 21.g4 is worth a shot.

If Black gobbles the pawn at f2 then the f-file can be used to get a rook to the 8th rank,) 14...fxe6 and Black threatens to get in ...Qh5 and chase away the only defender of the pawn at g7. White may have to part with the a-pawn to prevent this. 15.Nf4 (15.Nd4 Qxa2; 16.Nxe6 transposes.) 15...Qxa2; 16.Nxe6 (16.Ng5 Qa1+; 17.Kd2 Qxb2; 18.Nfxe6 Qc3+; 19.Ke2 Qxc2+; 20.Rd2 Qc4+; 21.Rd3 Rc8 leaves White with nothing to show for the material.) 16...Qxe6; 17.Nxd6+ exd6; 18.Rhe1 Qxe1; 19.Rxe1+ Kd7; 20.Re4 c5; 21.Rf4 a5; 22.Rf7+ Kc6 and Black should win by advancing the a-pawn.

B2) 13...Qh5? is a serious mistake because of 14.Bg5! Qg4; 15.Nf4 d5; 16.Bxd5 cxd5; 17.Nxd5 f5; 18.Nef6+ exf6; 19.Nxf6+ Kf7; 20.Nxg4 fxg4; 21.Rhe1 Be6; 22.Rd7+ and faced with mate in 6, Black resigned, Vodicka – Djurkovic, Hradec Kralove 1992.

C) 10...d5 leads to the natural 11.0-0-0 Qb6; (11...e5; 12.f4 Be6; 13.Ne4 f6; 14.fxe5 fxe5; 15.Rhf1 takes control of f6 and delivers a big advantage to White, Schroder – Haeusler, Germany 1981.) 12.Bxd5 cxd5; 13.Nxd5 Qa5 was agreed drawn after 14.a3 in Peters – Faelten, USA 1979, but John Nunn shows White getting a huge advantage after 14.b4! Qa3+; 15.Kb1 Bd7; 16.Rd3 Qa4; 17.Nc7+ Kd8; 18.Nxa8.

SHORT ATTACK: PART ONE, MOVE 9
Option 2: 9...Bf5

A move that is worthy of further investigation.

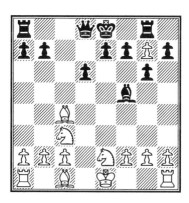

10.Nd4 e5; 11.Nf3 c6; 12.Bg5 Qb6; 13.0-0-0 Qb4 (13...Qxf2; 14.Nd4! is messy.) 14.Bb3 h6; 15.Bxh6 Be6; 16.Bxe6 fxe6; 17.Rhe1 d5; 18.Rxe5 0-0-0; 19.Nd4 and White went on to win in Claesen – Ng, Australia 1988.

SHORT ATTACK: PART ONE, MOVE 9
Option 3: 9...c5
The idea of playing on the queenside is simply wrong, as the Black king quickly comes under assault.

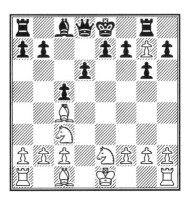

10.Bh6 Bd7; 11.0-0-0 Bc6 is much too slow. After 12.Nf4 Qd7; 13.Rhe1 Black's thrashing around on the queenside is useless. 13...b5; 14.Bd5 e6; 15.Bxe6 fxe6; 16.Rxe6+ Qxe6; 17.Nxe6 Ke7; 18.Nf8 Rd8; 19.Bg5+ and Black resigned, De Jong – Schildhuizen, Utrecht 1982.

SHORT ATTACK: PART ONE, MOVE 9
Option 4: 9...e5
This leaves a gaping hole at f6.

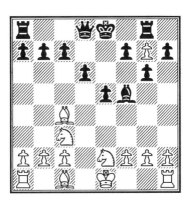

10.Ne4 is virtually winning for White. If Black grabs the pawn, there is nothing "virtual" about it! 10...Rxg7??; 11.Bg5 and Black must resign, Pape – Noer, Denmark 1987.

Returning to the Main Line
10.Bh6 Rg8; 11.0–0–0.

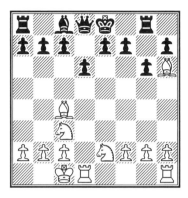

White has racked up a tremendous score from this position, which computers evaluate as clearly better for Black. How can we explain this? The answer lies in the Black pawns. If they stay in place there is no way to get the rooks into the game. But if they advance, they create holes which can be exploited by Black's minor pieces. The result is a position which is very difficult to play for Black.

11...Be6.

John Nunn, one of the greatest authorities on the Pirc, considers this the best move so we adopt it as our main line. Be sure to examine alternatives that remain in circulation, because they do surface from time to time. These involve similar plans to those at move 9.

Defensive players may want to cover up with 11...e6. Black can prepare to advance the d-pawn by playing 11...c6. The center can be brought under control with 11...e5. The bishop can be stationed at f5.

SHORT ATTACK: PART ONE - OPTIONS AT MOVE 11

Option 1: 11...e6
Option 2: 11...c6
Option 3: 11...e5
Option 4: 11...Bf5

SHORT ATTACK: PART ONE, MOVE 11
Option 1: 11...e6

Black seeks to cover up, but this solid approach doesn't address the kingside issues.

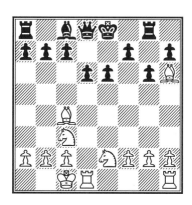

12.h4 is the correct reaction.

A) 12...Bd7 is the best move. 13.Ne4 f6; 14.Nf4 and here

A1) 14...Qe7; 15.Rhe1 0-0-0; 16.Nxe6 Bxe6; 17.Nc3 d5; 18.Nxd5 Qc5; 19.Ne7+ Kb8; 20.Nxg8 Rxd1+; 21.Rxd1 Qxc4; 22.b3 (22.Rd8+ Bc8; 23.Be3 would have made it difficult for Black to achieve anything. Whether White can make progress is equally unclear.) 22...Qc3; 23.Rd8+ Bc8; 24.Re8 Qa1+; 25.Kd2 Qd4+; 26.Ke1 Qd7; 27.Nxf6 Qc6; 28.Rf8 b6; 29.c4 Kb7 is Dabrowska – Deglmann, German Junior Championship 1993. Here instead of 30.g4, White should play 30.Kf1 and work on Black's kingside pawns.

A2) 14...Kf7; 15.Rhe1 Re8; 16.g4 a5; 17.a3 b5; 18.Ba2 Re7; 19.g5 f5; 20.Nf6 Bc8; 21.Nxh7 c5; 22.h5 gxh5; 23.g6+ Kg8; 24.Nf6+ Kh8; 25.Nxe6 and Black resigned, Short – Miles, London 1977.

B) 12...a6; 13.Ne4 f6; 14.Nf4 g5; 15.hxg5 fxg5; 16.Bxe6 Bxe6; 17.Nxe6 and White was much better in Motta – Stacey, Montana 1990.

C) 12...Qe7; 13.Nf4 c6; 14.Ne4 d5; 15.Bg5 Qc7; 16.Nf6+ Kf8; 17.Bh6+ Rg7; 18.Bxd5 cxd5; 19.Bxg7+ Ke7; 20.N4xd5+ exd5; 21.Nxd5+ Kd7; 22.Nxc7+ Kxc7; 23.Be5+ Kb6; 24.Rd8 and Black resigned, Sciacca – Schalk, Queen Open 1996.

SHORT ATTACK: PART ONE, MOVE 11
Option 2: 11...c6

White should respond to this plan by lining up the big guns in the center.

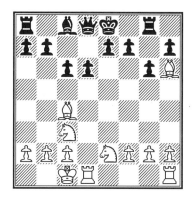

12.Rhe1. Our forces are in place, and it is just about time to blast open the center. 12...d5 (12...Qc7; 13.Nf4 g5; 14.Ne4 gxf4; 15.Nxd6+ Kd8; 16.Nxf7+ Ke8; 17.Nd6+ Qxd6; 18.Rxd6 Rxg2; 19.Bxf4 Rxf2; 20.Bg5 Bf5; 21.Rxe7+ was the brutal conclusion to Jahr – Kraus, Nurenberg 1990.) 13.Nxd5!? Suddenly Black's defensive barrier is gone. 13...cxd5; 14.Rxd5 Bd7; 15.Nc3. Although we only have two pieces for the queen, we can exploit the position of the Black king to regain some material. Black can try to play on the kingside or on the queenside.

A) 15...g5; 16.Bxg5 Rxg5; 17.Rxg5 Kf8; 18.Re3. Black is falling into a bad position, and White has enough material for the queen. 18...Qc7; 19.Reg3 Qf4+; 20.Kb1 e6; 21.Rg8+ Ke7; 22.Rxa8 and White went on to win in Chernitsyn – Berezovics, Ekaterinburg 1996.

B) 15...Qb6; 16.Rde5 e6; 17.Nd5. Black has nothing better than 17...Qxf2; 18.Nc7+ Ke7; 19.Bg5+ Kd6; 20.Nxa8 Rxa8; 21.R5e2. Now we have a rook and bishop for the queen and a pawn, but the Black rook is still inactive and the king is exposed. 21...Qf5; 22.Rd2+ Kc6; 23.Be7 and the position remains unclear.)

SHORT ATTACK: PART ONE, MOVE 11
Option 3: 11...e5
This pawn quickly becomes a target for White's attack.

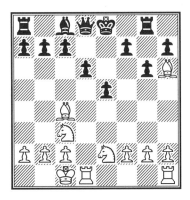

12.f4 exf4; 13.Ne4 g5; 14.h4 gxh4; 15.Nxf4 Bf5. Now a series of blows pummels the Black king into submission. 16.Bb5+ Ke7; 17.Nd5+ Ke6; 18.Nc5+ dxc5; 19.Rhe1+ Be4; 20.Rxe4+ Kf5; 21.Ne7+ Kxe4; 22.Re1+ Kd4; 23.c3# McAlpine – Lumsden, Postal 1974. This is one of the earliest examples of the Short Attack.

SHORT ATTACK: PART ONE, MOVE 11
Option 4: 11...Bf5
The bishop comes under fire after **12.Nd4!**

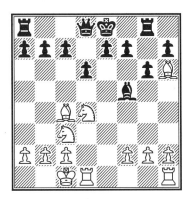

The goal here is not so much to attack the bishop, as to centralize the knight and keep an eye on the e6-square. 12...e5 (12...Qd7; 13.Rhe1 0-0-0; 14.Bxf7 e5; 15.Bxg8 Rxg8; 16.Nd5. White had gained the upper hand in Weiner – Schwarzburger, Germany 1989.) 13.Nf3 Be6; 14.Bxe6 fxe6; 15.Ne4 Rh8; 16.Bg5 Qb8; 17.Nxe5 Rf8; 18.Ng4 and White was clearly better in Kindermann – Gass, Germany 1978.

12.Bxe6 fxe6.

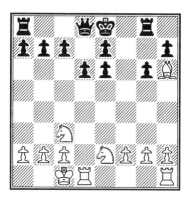

This position has been reached a number of times, and White has had time to figure out the most effective plan.

13.Rhe1! The e-file may seem blocked by pieces both friendly and unfriendly, but it is where the action will take place! **13...Qd7; 14.Nf4 e5; 15.Rxe5.**

The e-pawn was lost in any case.

15...Qg4. 15...dxe5; 16.Rxd7 Kxd7; 17.Nd3. The e-pawn is not going anywhere. 17...Rad8; 18.Ne4 Kc8; 19.f3 Rd4; 20.h4. White is slowly torturing his opponent, waiting until just the right moment to grab the e-pawn. 20...b6; 21.b3 c5; 22.Bg5 Re8; 23.Nxe5. Finally! White's three minor pieces are more than a match for the rooks, which have nothing to do. 23...Rd5; 24.Nc4 Kb7; 25.Ne3 Rd7; 26.c4 a5; 27.a4 Kc6. Black has run out of meaningful moves. 28.Kc2 Rb7; 29.Nd5 Ra7; 30.Be3 Rd7; 31.Ng5 Kb7; 32.Bf4. Black either resigned or, more likely, lost on time in Weinwurm – Stadtmuller, Merano 1988.

16.f3 Qd7; 17.Ne6 dxe5; 18.Rxd7 Kxd7; 19.Nc5+ Kc6; 20.Nd3 Kd6.

Black's rooks are useless here and White slowly squeezes a win out of the position. **21.Ne4+ Kd5; 22.Bd2 h6; 23.Nb4+ Ke6; 24.Nc5+ Kf7; 25.Nxb7 g5; 26.h3 h5.** If Black can eliminate all the kingside pawns there are good drawing chances. But White does not have to cooperate! **27.Nc5 g4; 28.fxg4 hxg4; 29.h4! Rad8; 30.Nbd3 Rd5; 31.c4 Rdd8; 32.Nxe5+ Kf6; 33.Ncd3 Kf5; 34.Bg5 Ke4; 35.Kd2 Rg7; 36.Nxg4** and White won without much difficulty in Sieg–Schoeneich, Bundesliga 1996.

PIRC DEFENSE
Short Attack (Part Two)

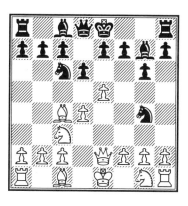

OPENING MOVES	
1.e4	d6
2.d4	Nf6
3.Nc3	g6
4.Bc4	Bg7
5.Qe2	Nc6
6.e5	Ng4

OVERVIEW

Moving the knight to g4 in the **Short Attack** has traditionally been a popular option for Black. Black's knight is not really vulnerable at g4 and has no intention of staying there for long. The e-pawn is under attack and something must be done about it.

Not surprisingly, we have a sharp gambit line in mind. The light squares in the enemy forecourt, particularly e6 and f7, are rather weak. We will advance our e-pawn to e6 in order to force Black to permanently weaken the squares further.

Then we have another sacrifice in mind. We are going to let Black's knight travel from c6 to d4, check on c2, and capture our rook at a1. That is a time-consuming maneuver, and we will put our extra time to good use!

PIRC DEFENSE	
Short Attack: Part Two	
7.e6 Nxd4	
Options at move 7	*130*
Option 1: 7...d5	130
Option 2: 7...f5	131

7.e6!? This disrupts communication between the bishop at c8 and knight at g4, which is now unprotected. White will sacrifice more material, including the rook at a1. This line is definitely not for the fainthearted. A less risky alternative is 7.Bb5, which leads to a roughly level game.

7...Nxd4. The two alternatives are insufficient for equality. By-passing the pawn on the d-file and f-file have been tried. Lets look at two options.

SHORT ATTACK: PART TWO - OPTIONS AT MOVE 7

1.e4 d6; 2.d4 Nf6; 3.Nc3 g6; 4.Bc4 Bg7; 5.Qe2 Nc6; 6.e5 Ng4; 7.e6
Option 1: 7...d5
Option 2: 7...f5

SHORT ATTACK: PART TWO, MOVE 7
Option 1: 7...d5

Black dares to try to deprive our bishop from performing its ceremonial and military duties. We can't let that happen! So, not worrying about our rook at a1, we will play a forcing continuation.

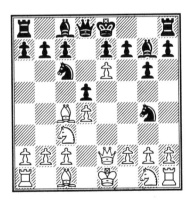

8.Bxd5! leads to 8...Nxd4; 9.Qxg4 Nxc2+; 10.Ke2 Nxa1.

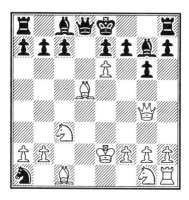

This is a very exciting line with great complications. 11.exf7+ Kf8; 12.Qh4 Nc2; 13.Nf3 h5; 14.Rd1 Bg4; 15.Kf1 Bxf3; 16.Bxf3 Nd4; 17.Bxb7 Rb8; 18.Bd5 c5 is Bezemer – Piket, Amsterdam 1986. I think that after 19.Bc4, pinning the knight, White has some promising play against the weak pawn at g6 that fully compensates for the exchange.

SHORT ATTACK: PART TWO, MOVE 7
Option 2: 7...f5

We are invited to lock the central door by advancing the d-pawn.

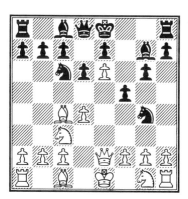

Nunn dismisses 8.d4 on the basis of 8...Nd4, but Black has another option we must consider, too. We'll start with the main line.

A) 8...Nd4; 9.Qd1 c6; 10.h3 Ne5 (10...b5; 11.hxg4 bxc4; 12.Bh6 was very strong for White in Farrand – J. Littlewood, Postal 1977.) 11.Qxd4! This queen sacrifice is so powerful that Black does not survive for long. 11...Nf3+; 12.Nxf3 Bxd4; 13.Nxd4 Qb6; 14.Nde2 0–

0. White's advantage in space and the closed nature of the position make it difficult for the Black queen to be effective and the other pieces are useless. 15.Bh6 Re8; 16.0-0 Qb4; 17.Bb3 Qh4; 18.Be3.

Now Black makes the fatal error of opening up the kingside, a plan which can only be described as stupid. How can Black even dream of an attack with only the queen in the game? 18...g5?; 19.f4 g4; 20.hxg4 fxg4; 21.Ne4 Qh6; 22.Ng5. Black is doomed. White just plays f5 and breaks through. White won in Timmerman–Goudsword, Papendrecht Fokker 1990.

B) 8...Na5 attacks the bishop at c4. White need not fear the exchange of this piece and can attend to the rest of the development process. 9.h3 Nf6; 10.Nf3 c6; 11.0-0 0-0; 12.Ng5 b5; 13.Nf7 Rxf7; 14.exf7+ Kxf7. The position is exciting, but objectively I'd rate the chances as about even. 15.Bb3 b4; 16.Nd1 cxd5; 17.Qb5 Nxb3; 18.axb3 a5; 19.Be3 Bd7; 20.Qb6 Qc8; 21.Rxa5 Rb8; 22.Qa7 Bb5 was drawn in Belaska – Pribyl, Prague 1994.

Returning to the Main Line

So, we are left with the main line, **7...Nxd4**, which deflects the queen from c2.

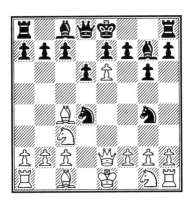

This leads to **8.Qxg4 Nxc2+; 9.Kf1.**

We now have the sort of position any gambiteer must love. Sure you will lose the rook at a1, but the pressure at f7 is intense and White's pieces have plenty of room to roam.

9...Nxa1. 9...f5 is not mentioned by Nunn, but it is a serious alternative to the immediate capture. 10.Qd1 (10.Qe2 Nxa1; 11.Nf3 c6; 12.Ng5 Qb6) 10...Nxa1; 11.Bf4 c6; 12.Nf3 d5; 13.Bd3 Bxe6; 14.Qxa1 0-0 15.h4.

Does White have enough compensation? Black has a rook and three pawns for two pieces. White will have to blast open the kingside to succeed. It is important to note that the Black rooks have no real scope. White will be able to occupy e5 and can bring all of the pieces to the kingside. Only practical tests will determine whether there are sufficient resources to complete the job.

9...Bxe6?? overlooks a tactical trap. 10.Bxe6 fxe6; 11.Qa4+ and Black resigned, De Jong – Westerhuis, Postal 1989.

10.exf7+ Kf8; 11.Qh4.

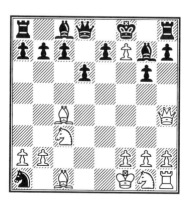

11...d5. 11...h6 (11...c6?; 12.Bh6 d5; 13.Qd4 wins, as pointed out by Nunn. 11...b5 has been suggested, but after 12.Bd5 Rb8; 13.Bh6 c5; 14.Nge2 Nc2; 15.Nf4 White still has a strong attack, despite the material disadvantage.) 12.Nge2 g5 (12...d5 is unclear, according to Nunn. 13.Bxd5 c6; 14.Be4 Kxf7; 15.Qf4+ Bf6; 16.Qg3 Bf5; 17.Bxf5 gxf5; 18.Nf4 Qg8; 19.Qd3 and White will eventually pick up the knight at a1, with compensation.) 13.Qh5 e6; 14.h4 Qf6; 15.Rh3 g4; 16.Re3 Nc2; 17.Re4 e5; 18.Nf4 Bf5; 19.Ncd5 Qxf7; 20.Qxf7+ Kxf7; 21.Ne3+ Kf8; 22.Nxf5 exf4; 23.Nxg7 Kxg7; 24.Bd3 and the Black knight cannot be saved; if it goes back to a1, White plays b4 and Bb2+. White went on to win in Van der Plassche – Piket, Hilversum 1985.

12.Bxd5 c6. 12...Bxc3; 13.Bh6+ Bg7; 14.Qd4 (14.Bxg7+ Kxg7; 15.Qd4+ fails to 15...e5; 16.Qxe5+ Qf6.) 14...e5;15.Qxe5 Bxh6; 16.Qxh8+ Ke7; 17.Qe5+ draws, following analysis by Nunn.

13.Bh6. 13.Be4 Kxf7; 14.Nf3 provides "continuing complications", according to Nunn. There is nothing complicated about 14...Bxc3 which leaves Black a rook ahead, since the bishop cannot be captured: 15.bxc3 Qd1+; 16.Ne1 Qxc1 etc. **13...Nc2.**

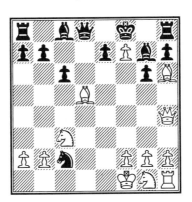

13...Qd6; 14.Bc4 (Not 14.Bf4?? e5 where White felt compelled to resign in Koch – Ganesan, Postal 1990). 14...b5; 15.Bxg7+ Kxg7; 16.Be2 Kxf7; 17.Nf3 and the position is still very complicated.

14.Be4. 14.Bc4 does not work because of 14...Qd4!; 14.Qf4!? cxd5; (14...Qd6 is a better defense.) 15.Qe5 Kxf7; 16.Qxg7+ Ke6; 17.Nf3 is an interesting alternative which might be good for White.

14...Nd4; 15.g4. 15.Nge2 Nxe2; 16.Kxe2 Kxf7; 17.Rd1 Qc7. Black is better. **15...Be6; 16.Nh3 Bxf7; 17.Kg2 e5; 18.Ng5 Kg8; 19.Rd1 Qf6.**

White could find no way to make progress in Isonzo – Belotti Italian Championship 1996. This is the latest word on the variation.

PIRC DEFENSE
Short Attack: (Part Three)

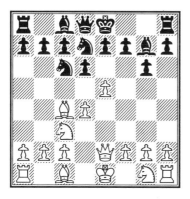

OPENING MOVES	
1.e4	d6
2.d4	Nf6
3.Nc3	g6
4.Bc4	Bg7
5.Qe2	Nc6
6.e5	Nd7

The knight's retreat to d7 in this continuation of the **Short Attack** (Part 3) is a move with a deservedly solid reputation. Black plays in true hypermodern style and puts pressure on the pawn at e5.

Here we must show some patience. It is essential to win the battle for the e5-square. That's really all you need to remember. You must also provide some support for the extended pawn. If you can do that, then Black will suffer from lack of space and your control of the center will allow you to maneuver your pieces freely. Exploit that by swinging your pieces to the center and then to the kingside, and you will be able to attack!

There are two remaining alternatives to the retreat of the knight: Black can move the knight to h5, or Black can capture the pawn at d5. We'll consider those two moves on the way to the main lines.

PIRC DEFENSE
Short Attack: Part Three
Continuation

Options at move 6	136
Option 1: 6...Nh5	136
Option 2: 6...dxe5	137

SHORT ATTACK: PART THREE - OPTIONS AT MOVE 6

Option 1: 6...Nh5
Option 2: 6...dxe5

SHORT ATTACK: PART THREE, MOVE 6
Option 1: 6...Nh5

The knight is a sitting target on this square.

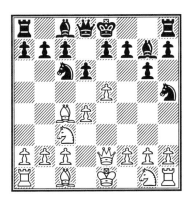

7.Bb5 0–0; 8.Bxc6 bxc6.

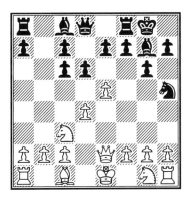

White already has a serious advantage, as it will be easy to create a kingside attack. 9.g4 dxe5; (9...c5; 10.dxc5 Bb7; 11.Nf3 Qd7; 12.Rg1 Qc6; 13.Nd4 Qxc5; 14.Nb3 led to a win for White in Short – Botterill,

London 1978.) 10.dxe5 Bxg4; 11.Qxg4 Bxe5; 12.Nf3 Bxc3+; 13.bxc3 Qd5; 14.0–0 and White consolidated his advantage in Shubert – Pedersen, Groningen 1978.

SHORT ATTACK: PART THREE, MOVE 6
Option 2: 6...dxe5

Black tries to relieve the pressure on the e-file, but there is more to come!

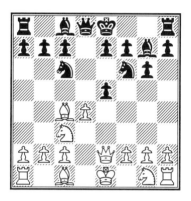

7.dxe5 Ng4; 8.e6!

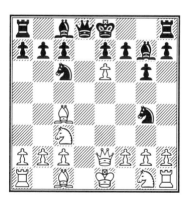

This move destroys the communication between Black's minor pieces and leads to a strong game for White.

A) 8...Nd4; 9.exf7+ Kf8; 10.Qd1 Bf5; 11.Bd3 Qd7 (11...Kxf7; 12.Bxf5 gxf5; 13.h3 Ne5; 14.Be3 gives White the initiative.) 12.Nge2 Rd8; 13.f3 Ne5; 14.Bxf5 Qxf5; 15.Nxd4 Rxd4; 16.Qe2 Kxf7; 17.Be3 and White is slightly better thanks to the healthier pawn structure,

Zajontz – Deuster, Postal 1990.
B) 8...f5; 9.Nf3 Nd4; 10.Nxd4 Bxd4; (10...Qxd4; 11.Nb5 Qc5; 12.Bf4 Be5; 13.Bxe5 Nxe5; 14.Bb3 a6; 15.Nc3 b5; 16.Bd5 Nc6; 17.Rd1 Bb7; 18.0-0 gave White the more active game in De Jong – Leentfaar, Netherlands 1982.) 11.f3.

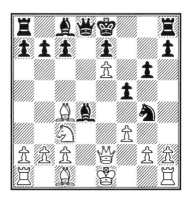

Here neither retreat is fully satisfactory for Black. 11...Nf6 (11...Ne5; 12.Bf4 Bxc3+; 13.bxc3 Nxc4; 14.Qxc4 leaves Black very cramped, for example 14...c6; 15.Be5 0-0; 16.0-0 Qd5; 17.Qf4 Bxe6; 18.Rad1 Qc4; 19.Rd4 Qc5; 20.h4 Rad8; 21.h5 Rf7; 22.hxg6 hxg6; 23.Qh6 and Black resigned in Shulbskis – Kutsukhidse, Simferopol 1990.) 12.Bh6 Bxc3+; 13.bxc3 c6; 14.Bg7 Rf8; 15.Bxf8 Kxf8; 16.Rd1 and Black was in serious trouble in Ongarelli – Siviero, Italy 1985.

Returning to the Main Line

We are finished with all the reasonable tries at move six except one: **6...Nd7**, which puts a lot of pressure at e5.

7.Nf3 White must not try rash moves such as e6 or Bxf7+ here. They simply do not work. **7...Nb6.** Two other moves come into consideration:

A) 7...0-0 is a sensible alternative. But here, too, we can mix things up with 8.e6!?

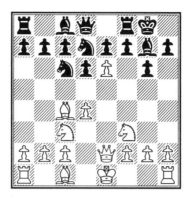

8...fxe6; 9.Bxe6+ Kh8; 10.Be3 Nb6 (10...Rxf3; 11.Qxf3 Nxd4; 12.Bxd4 Bxd4 is insufficient after the simple 13.0-0-0, for example: 13...Ne5; 14.Qd5 Bxc3; 15.bxc3 Bertona – Olivieri, Buenos Aires 1993.) 11.Bxc8 Qxc8; 12.0-0-0 e5; 13.d5 e4; 14.Ng5 Nb4; 15.a3 Bxc3; 16.axb4 Be5; 17.h4 h5; 18.Nxe4 c6; 19.dxc6 and White is much better, Short – Utasi, Sas van Gent 1979.

B) 7...dxe5 leads to a an interesting sacrifice: 8.Bxf7+ Kf8; 9.dxe5 Kxf7; 10.Ng5+ Ke8; 11.Ne6 Nd4; 12.Nxg7+ Kf8 was seen in Hablizel – Schulz, Dresden 1992 and here 13.Bh6!? is an interesting queen sacrifice. After 13...Nxe2; 14.Ne6+ Kf7; 15.Nxd8+ Rxd8; 16.Kxe2 Nxe5; 17.Bf4, White has a small positional advantage.

8.Bb3 0-0. 8...d5 leads to a position similar to the Alekhine Defense. White can get a small advantage but no more. 9.h3 0-0; 10.Bf4 Be6; 11.0-0-0 Rc8; 12.Qe3 Na5; 13.Ng5 Nbc4; 14.Qg3 c5; 15.Qh4 gave White a promising attack in Braeuning – Kowohl, Germany 1992. **9.h3.**

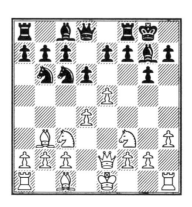

9...Na5. Opening up the center is a reasonable alternative. 9...dxe5; 10.dxe5 Nd4; 11.Nxd4 Qxd4; 12.f4 Be6; 13.Be3 Qd7; 14.Rd1 (14.0-0 Bxb3; 15.axb3 Qc6; 16.Ra5 Rfd8; 17.Rd1 is a good alternative, Kveinis – Zimmerman, Polanica Zdroj 1992.) 14...Qc6; 15.0-0 Bxb3; 16.axb3 Rad8; 17.Kh1 f5; 18.Bxb6 axb6; 19.Qc4+ e6; 20.Nb5 Qxc4; 21.bxc4 was marginally better for White in De Kleuver – Van Parreren, Netherlands Women Championship 1990. **10.Bf4 d5.** 10...Nxb3; 11.axb3 dxe5 (11...Re8; 12.0-0 a6; 13.Rfd1 Bf5; 14.g4 allows White to develop an attack, De Jong – Van Wieringen, Postal 1992.) 12.Bxe5 f6; 13.Bg3 c6; 14.0-0 Nd5; 15.Rfe1 e6; 16.Ne4 gave White a slight advantage in space and mobility in De Jong – Veerman, Utrecht 1983. **11.0-0 h6; 12.Nd1 Be6; 13.c3 Nxb3; 14.axb3 Qd7.**

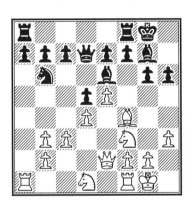

Nunn evaluates this position as equal, and that may be the case. Still, White has more space and can maneuver more quickly. Indeed the game Nunn cites turned out well for White after **15.Ne3 c6; 16.Ne1 f5; 17.exf6 exf6; 18.Nd3 Qf7; 19.Nc5 Rfe8; 20.Qd3 Bf8; 21.Nxe6 Rxe6; 22.Rfe1 Re4; 23.Bh2 a6; 24.f3 Re6; 25.Re2 Rae8; 26.Rae1 Nd7; 27.g4 Kh8; 28.Kg2 Bg7; 29.Bf4 Nf8; 30.h4 Kg8; 31.Rh1 Nh7; 32.h5 gxh5; 33.Rxh5 Ng5; 34.Rd2 Qf8; 35.Nf5 Kf7; 36.Rh1 Kg8; 37.Kg3 Re1; 38.Rdh2 Rxh1; 39.Rxh1 Kf7; 40.Nd6+ Kg8; 41.Qg6 Re2; 42.Nf5 Nf7; 43.Bxh6 Nxh6; 44.Nxh6+** and Black resigned, Soltis – Quinteros, Lone Pine 1979.

MODERN DEFENSE
• Foguelman Attack •

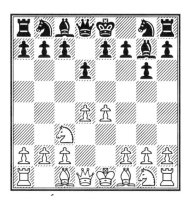

OPENING MOVE

1.e4	g6
2.d4	Bg7
3.Nc3	d6

OVERVIEW

The Modern Defense is a very popular opening. It appeals to many players because the opening is played almost on autopilot. Black intends ...g6, ...Bg7, ...d6, and then can choose from the Pirc or King's Indian, or more unusual strategies.

When Black's forces remain on the back three ranks, gambits are not easy to find. We are even more limited because we must beware of transpositions to the Pirc Defense. Fortunately, we can employ the same strategy as in the Short Attack, discussed in the previous three chapters. The game can transpose, or can take on a more original character, as we will see in the discussion in this section on the **Foguelman Attack**.

As long as you don't get carried away with crazy sacrifices, you should be able to build up an initiative which you can later turn into a fierce attack!

MODERN DEFENSE
Foguelman Attack

4.Bc4 Nc6

Options at move 4	142
Option 1: 4...c6	142
Option 2: 4...Nd7	143
Option 3: 4...e6	144
Option 4: 4...c5!?	145

4.Bc4 Nc6. 4...Nf6 returns to the Short Attack in the Pirc Defense, but there are other moves to be considered. Black can choose a variety of central strategies. The c-pawn can advance one square to support ...d5, or two, to undermine the control of d4. The dangerous diagonal can be sealed with 4...e6. Finally, the knight can be developed at d7.

FOGUELMAN ATTACK - OPTIONS AT MOVE 4

1.e4 g6; 2.d4 Bg7; 3.Nc3 d6; 4.Bc4 Nc6
Option 1: 4...c6
Option 2: 4...Nd7
Option 3: 4...e6
Option 4: 4...c5

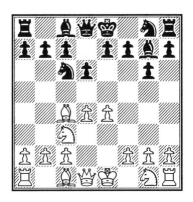

FOGUELMAN ATTACK, MOVE 4
Option 1: 4...c6

Black attempts to steer the game into rather boring lines of the Pirc but White can try to mix things up.

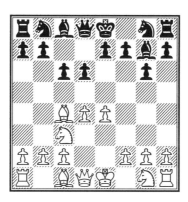

5.Qf3, for example, is part of a plan involving queenside castling. 5...e6; 6.Nge2 Nd7; 7.Be3 Ngf6; 8.Bb3 e5; 9.0-0-0.

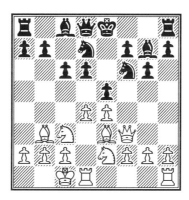

Black is more or less obligated to castle kingside at some point. That is one of the burdens of a kingside fianchetto. So the attacks will flare up on opposite flanks. 9...Qe7; 10.h3 a6; 11.g4! b5 and for some reason unfathomable by me, in Yegiazarian – Minasian, Armenian Championship 1996, White foolishly captured on e5 and gave Black a great outpost for free. Much better is 12.g5 Nh5; 13.Qg2 0-0; 14.f4, opening up the game.

FOGUELMAN ATTACK, MOVE 4
Option 2: 4...Nd7

Black can use this move to discourage White from playing f4, which can now be met by ...e5!

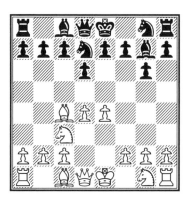

5.Nf3 Ngf6 (5...Nh6; 6.h3 a6; 7.Be3 e6; 8.0–0 Ng8; 9.a4 Ne7 is an artificial plan seen in Neugebauer – Patiens, Nurmeburg 1996. 10.Qd2 would have given White a good kingside attack.) 6.Bg5 0–0 is Bitros – Valden, Aegina 1996, and here instead of the premature advance of the e-pawn, White should have either castled kingside or played Qe2 with an eye toward queenside castling.

FOGUELMAN ATTACK, MOVE 4
Option 3: 4...e6
Slow, solid, and not very good. White grabs the c1-h6 diagonal.

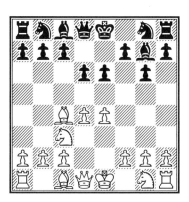

5.Be3 Ne7; 6.Qd2 h6 weakens the kingside. After 7.0–0–0 White will get a good game. If Black attempts to build a queenside attack, the domination of the center by White will limit its effectiveness. For example, 7...a6; 8.f4. The simple 8.Nf3 might have been better. 8...b5; 9.Bb3 c6 as in Lukasiewicz – Bricard, Cannes 1996, where 10.g4 a5;

11.a4 would have been strong.

FOGUELMAN ATTACK, MOVE 4
Option 4: 4...c5!?
Black tries to steer the game into a Sicilian Defense. That is a good plan.

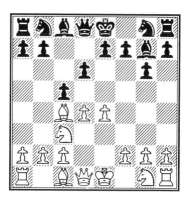

5.Nge2 (or 5.Nf3) 5...cxd4; 6.Nxd4 brings the game into Sicilian territory. 6...Nf6; 7.0-0 0-0 is a line from the Classical Dragon. The basic ideas for White are h3, Be3, Bb3, Kh1, and f4.

Instead, White might try 5.Be3.

Returning to the Main Line
Let's return to the main line after **4...Nc6.**

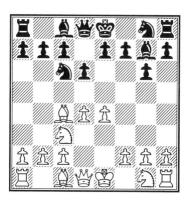

Developing the knight on the queenside is the most common alternative to 4...Nf6.

5.Nf3. Foguelmann's original idea, against Incutto at Buenos Aires 1959, was to play 5.Nge2. The knight stands better at f3. **5...Nf6.**

We are back in a Pirc where Black is committed to the formation with ...Nc6. Now we can set up a similar formation to the one used against that opening by playing Be3, but first we need to keep an enemy piece off of g4. **6.h3 0–0; 7.Qe2 Nd7.** 7...e5; 8.dxe5 dxe5; 9.Bg5 creates an annoying pin. This was suggested by Nunn as an improvement on Povah – Nunn, England 1977. **8.Be3 e5.** 8...Nb6; 9.Bd3! Nb4; 10.0–0 c6; 11.Qd2 Nxd3; 12.cxd3 gives White an impressive pawn mass in the center. 12...Re8; 13.Bh6 Bh8; 14.Ne2 e5. M.Gurevich – Temmink, Uebach 1996. 15.dxe5 dxe5; 16.a4 is dynamically balanced, with White operating on the queenside and Black concentrating on the weakness at d3. Black has a terrible bishop at h8. **9.Rd1 exd4; 10.Nxd4 Nce5 11.Bb3.** We have an unusual line that might have arisen from a Philidor Defense. **11...Nc5; 12.0–0 Nxb3; 13.axb3.**

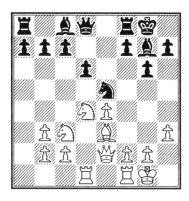

The double pawns are not significant. Black has the bishop pair but the light-squared bishop has no place to go. **13...Nc6; 14.Nxc6 bxc6; 15.f4 Re8; 16.Qc4** is a bit more comfortable for White, Medvegy – Seifert, Oberwart 1996.

CZECH DEFENSE

OPENING MOVES

1.e4   d6
2.d4   Nf6
3.Nc3   c6

OVERVIEW

The **Czech Defense** has become popular in recent years and, as is typical of a slow opening, it is hard to find a good gambit continuation against it.

Black intends to play ...e5 and transpose into an Open Game where White has forsaken all hope of an early gambit attack. If White plays quietly, however, then Black can transpose into slow and boring lines of the Pirc Defense.

How can we outwit our opponent and get a lively game? We must go for the jugular by advancing the f-pawn to punish Black for neglecting the center. Of course, Black will still try to get the pawn to e5. If properly timed, this can be an effective counter. White must prevent that freeing maneuver, unless it is carried out at a serious disadvantage.

If you can control the action at the e5 square, Black will find life miserable!

CZECH DEFENSE	
4. f4 Qa5	
Options at move 4	*149*
Option 1: 4...Bg4	149
Option 2: 4...Qc7	150
Option 3: 4...Nbd7	151
Option 4: 4...e6	152
Option 5: 4...d5	152
Option 6: 4...Qb6	153
Option 7: 4...e5	154
Option 8: 4...g6	155
5.e5 Ne4	
Option at move 5	*157*
Option 1: 5...Nd5	157
6.Bd3 Nxc3	
Options at move 6	*159*
Option 1: 6...f5	159
Option 2: 6...Bf5	159
7. Qd2	
Option at move 7	*161*
Option 1: 7...e6	161
Option 2: 7...d5	162
Option 3: 7...g6	163
Option 4: 7...g5	163
Option 5: 7...Qd5	164
Option 6: 7...c5!?	164
Option 7: 7...dxe5	165

4.f4 Qa5. This is the main line. Black supports the ...e5 advance from the flank. There are no less than eight reasonable alternatives! So White has to be prepared for a total of nine different moves, but the main point is that the center is dominated, and the task is primarily one of developing sensibly and keeping control of the center.

Black has tried attacking the queen with a bishop at g4, developing the queen to c7 or b6, and developing with 4...Nbd7. There are also four popular pawn moves. Preparing a kingside fianchetto by advancing the pawn to g6 leads to a Pirc Defense. The e-pawn can advance to e6 to take up a defensive position, or two squares, in an act of unbridled aggression. Finally, there is the blocking move 4...d5.

Let's look at each of these alternatives before returning to the main line.

CZECH DEFENSE - OPTIONS AT MOVE 4

<u>1.e4 d6; 2.d4 Nf6; 3.Nc3 c6; 4.f4 Qa5</u>
Option 1: 4...Bg4
Option 2: 4...Qc7
Option 3: 4...Nbd7
Option 4: 4...e6
Option 5: 4...d5
Option 6: 4...Qb6
Option 7: 4...e5
Option 8: 4...g6

CZECH DEFENSE, MOVE 4
Option 1: 4...Bg4

Black develops with tempo and prepares to exchange bishop for whatever piece interposes on the diagonal.

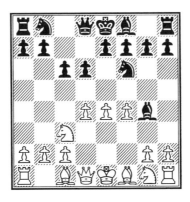

The queen is attacked, but finds a nice new home with **5.Qd3!**

The early queen move is justified here, as d3 is a safe square. Why allow Black to exchange pieces and ease the defensive burden? 5...Na6; 6.h3 Bd7; 7.Nf3 g6; 8.g4 looks a bit expansive, but Black had the worst of it in Schmidt–Westphal, Germany 1991 after 8...Bg7; 9.Be3 Qa5; 10.Qd2 and Black's king has reason to worry whichever way he castles.

CZECH DEFENSE, MOVE 4
Option 2: 4...Qc7

This is a very slow plan.

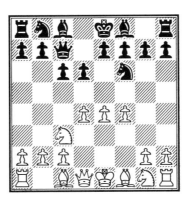

White can gain the bishop pair after 5.Nf3 Bg4; 6.h3 Bxf3; 7.Qxf3 e6.

White enjoys an advantage in space and can expand on the kingside. 8.g4 Nbd7; 9.Bd2 0-0-0; 10.0-0-0 Be7; 11.Kb1 is also more comfortable for White, especially if Black goes in for 11...d5?; 12.e5 Ne8; 13.f5!, as in Parma – Tsvetkov, Polanica Zdroj 1964.

CZECH DEFENSE, MOVE 4
Option 3: 4...Nbd7

This invites an advance in the center.

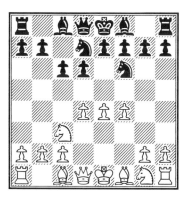

5.e5 Nd5; 6.Nf3 dxe5; 7.fxe5 e6.

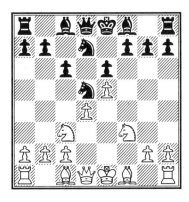

8.Ne4! Be7; 9.c4 gives White a strong initiative, Gazic – Sazonov, Ceske Budejovice 1992.

CZECH DEFENSE, MOVE 4
Option 4: 4...e6

This leaves Black with too cramped a position.

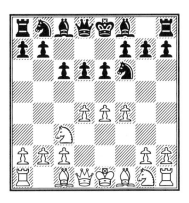

5.Nf3 Be7; 6.Bd3 0-0; 7.0–0 Nbd7; 8.e5 secures an advantage for White, Fleischer – Lotzwick, Postal 1980.

CZECH DEFENSE, MOVE 4
Option 5: 4...d5

The double step of the d-pawn is a waste of time, but it is not ridiculous. Black aims for a Gurgenidze Defense, where time is rarely a factor. White will enjoy an advantage in space, but the plans with f4 are not among the most effective. So Black trades off one tempo in order to force White into a position which is not as promising as the main lines of the Gurgenidze.

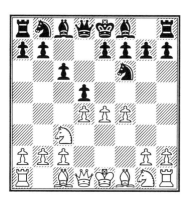

5.e5 Ng8 (5...Ne4; 6.Nxe4 dxe4; 7.Bc4 e6; 8.Ne2 b5; 9.Bb3 Bb7; 10.0-0 left Black's pawn structure shattered and gave White a strong initiative in Pinheiro – Farinha, Portugal 1993. 5...Ng4; 6.Bd3 Nh6; 7.Nf3 f5 is a bizarre plan, and after 8.Ng5 e6; 9.h3 Nf7; 10.g4! Nxg5; 11.fxg5 White had a strong position in Almasi–Nikolaidis, Balatonbereny 1994.)

6.Bd3 g6; 7.f5! Finally, a gambit! **7...Bxf5; 8.Bxf5 gxf5; 9.Qh5** White sets up the threat of e6, so Black gets there first. **9...e6; 10.Nf3 Nd7; 11.0-0 Ne7.** Black must adopt this awkward formation because neither f6 nor c6 are accessible to the knights.

12.Bg5. White has plenty of compensation for the pawn, Purgin – Vorotnikov, Belgrade 1989.

CZECH DEFENSE, MOVE 4
Option 6: 4...Qb6

This is a sensible plan. Black prevents the White bishop from developing because the pawn at b2 will fall. This is not a poisoned pawn but a tasty morsel!

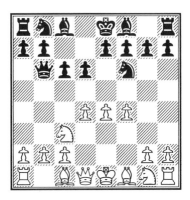

Normally White develops one of the kingside minor pieces here, but we'll let loose a more direct attack. **5.e5!? Nd5; 6.Nxd5 cxd5; 7.Bd3 g6.** Naturally we are going to try to attack on the f -file, but first we must attend to the hanging d-pawn.

8.c3 Bf5 (8...h5 is just weakening, and here is an example of the dangers that Black faces: 9.Qf3 Be6; 10.Nh3 Bxh3; 11.Qxh3 e6; 12.0–0 Nc6 and now 13.Bxg6!! fxg6; 14.Qxe6+ Ne7; 15.exd6 Rd8; 16.Qe5 forced Black's resignation in Sion Castro – Cabezas Ayala, Spain 1996.) **9.Bxf5 gxf5; 10.Nh3.** This is more subtle than 10.Qh5, and stronger. White stands better here, with only the bad bishop at c1 to worry about. Yet Black's bishop really isn't any better, because White has a Great Wall of pawns which keeps the enemy bishop from getting into the game. **10...h5.** A move designed to keep the queen off of h5, but it allows White to cause further damage to Black's structure.

11.e6!? (11.Qa4+ Qc6; 12.Qxc6+ Nxc6; 13.exd6 exd6 is a quieter path, but White certainly looks better here.) **11...fxe6; 12.Ng5 Rh6; 13.Qe2 Qa6; 14.Qe3!** There will be no exchange of queens. **14...Nd7; 15.Nxe6 Rc8; 16.Ng5 Bg7; 17.Qh3 e6; 18.Kd1 Nf8; 19.Re1 Kd7; 20.Bd2** and chances were about even in Sutovskij – Hodgson, Yerevan Olympiad 1996.

CZECH DEFENSE, MOVE 4
Option 7: 4...e5
This is simply unsound. Black loses a pawn and goes into an endgame! Some people will try anything to get out of playing the main lines.

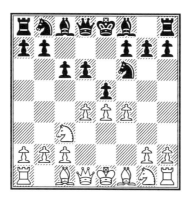

5.dxe5 dxe5; 6.Qxd8+ Kxd8; 7.fxe5 is crushing.

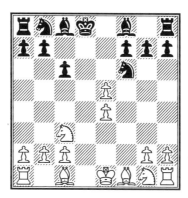

Black can't really expect to recover from this position. 7...Ng4 8.Nf3 Bc5; 9.Bc4 Ke7; 10.Ke2 Nd7; 11.Bg5+ f6; 12.exf6+ gxf6; 13.Bd2 consolidated White's position in Pedersen – Hoiberg, Randers 1996.

CZECH DEFENSE, MOVE 4
Option 8: 4...g6

The fianchetto transposes back to a Pirc, but ...c6 is not really appropriate against the f4 plans.

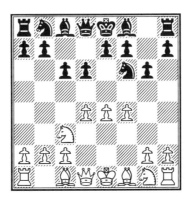

5.e5 Nd5 (5...Nfd7; 6.h4 c5; 7.exd6 exd6; 8.Qe2+ Qe7; 9.Nd5 Qxe2+; 10.Bxe2 Kd8; 11.Nf3 is a bit better for White, Hoffman – Cadavid, New York Open 1994. White has promising play against the weaknesses at d6, and f7, and can provoke more with a timely advance of the f-pawn.)

6.Ne4 Bg7; 7.c3 Bf5; 8.Bd3 Nc7; 9.Nf3 Bxe4; 10.Bxe4 d5; 11.Bc2 e6; 12.0–0.

White has more space, typical of the Gurgenidze Formation. The bishop pair is not of much use in a closed position, so White will try to open things up. Herzog – Nikolic, Vienna 1996.

Returning to the Main Line

So, we return to the main line with **4...Qa5**, which is by far the most popular move. **5.e5.**

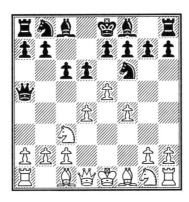

Again we choose the most active path. Black will not be allowed to achieve the goal of ...e5. Of course at the same time we are creating a pawn chain that will reduce the usefulness of the bishop at c1.

We'll look at the knight leap to e4 as our main line after exploring the knight move to d5.

CZECH DEFENSE - OPTION AT MOVE 5

1.e4 d6; 2.d4 Nf6; 3.Nc3 c6; 4.f4 Qa5; 5.e5
Option 1: 5...Nd5

CZECH DEFENSE, MOVE 5
Option 1: 5...Nd5

The knight does not sit well at d5.

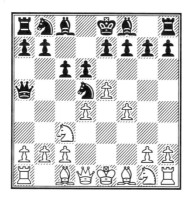

6.Bd2

A) 6...Qb6; 7.Bc4! is good for White, for example 7...dxe5; 8.Bxd5 cxd5; 9.fxe5 Qxd4; 10.Nf3 Qc5; 11.Qe2 Nc6; 12.Nb5 Qb6; 13.Be3 Qa5+ and now 14.b4! is an offer that must be refused. 14...Qxb4+ (14...Qd8; 15.0–0 a6; 16.Ng5 Be6; 17.Qf2 axb5; 18.Nxf7 Bxf7; 19.Bb6 was fatal in Votava – Tseshkovsky, Singapore 1990.) 15.Bd2 and Black can do nothing about the threat of Nc7+ and Nxa8.

B) 6...dxe5; 7.fxe5 Qb6; 8.Nf3 Bg4; 9.Na4 Qd8; 10.Nc5 b6; 11.Ne4 and White has a clear advantage, Andersson – Ufimtsev, Postal 1990.

C) 6...Nxc3; 7.Bxc3 Qd5.

Here White can get a small positional advantage with 8.Qf3, but that is hardly in the spirit of gambit play. 8.Nf3 Bf5; 9.Be2 is a more devious choice. White will just castle and then get ready for kingside action. If Black gets greedy, punishment is swift and certain. 9...Qe4?!; 10.0-0 Qxf4 lets White fire away and make the enemy queen dance like a poor fool in an old Western. 11.Bd2 Qg4; 12.exd6 exd6; 13.c3 frees the knight from the defense of the d-pawn. Black is way behind in development, and can't catch up, for example 13...Be7; 14.Ng5! Bc2!; 15.Qxc2 Qxe2; 16.Rae1 Qh5; 17.Rxf7.

Returning to the Main Line
   5...Ne4; 6.Bd3.

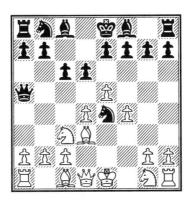

Are we overlooking the threat at c3? Hardly! **6...Nxc3.** Black falls into our trap. Not that supporting the knight with 6...f5 or 6...Bf5 is any better, as you can see.

CZECH DEFENSE - OPTIONS AT MOVE 6

1.e4 d6; 2.d4 Nf6; 3.Nc3 c6; 4.f4 Qa5; 5.e5 Ne4; 6.Bd3 Nxc3
Option 1: 6...f5
Option 2: 6...Bf5

CZECH DEFENSE, MOVE 6
Option 1: 6...f5

Black tries to support the knight, but the pawn can be eliminated by an *en passant* capture.

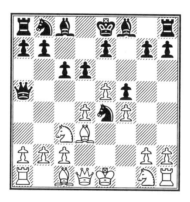

7.exf6 Nxf6; 8.Bd2 leaves Black with several problems. The forecourt is weak, especially e6, and White has a large lead in development. Surprise discovered attacks against the queen at a5 can turn nasty. 8...Na6; 9.a3 b5; 10.Nd5! Qd8; 11.Nxf6+ exf6 and here Black cannot even survive: 12.Qh5+ g6; 13.Bxg6+! Kd7; 14.Bf5+ Ke7; 15.0–0-0 Bg7; 16.Re1+ Kf8; 17.Ba5!! and the brilliant deflection ended the discussion in Sziebert – Francsics, Budapest 1996.

CZECH DEFENSE, MOVE 6
Option 2: 6...Bf5

Supporting the knight with the bishop does not work well either.

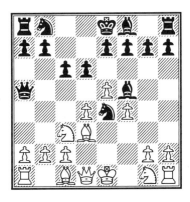

7.Qf3 Nxc3; 8.Bxf5! Nxa2+? (8...e6; 9.Bd2 exf5; 10.Bxc3 leaves Black at a serious spatial disadvantage.) 9.Bd2 Qa4; 10.Qa3! and Black cannot save the knight. So, none of the alternatives look very good.

Returning to the Main Line
Therefore we must concentrate on the capture with **6...Nxc3.** White now plays **7.Qd2.**

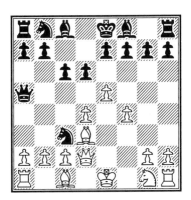

Black has tried a lot of moves here, but has found it difficult to achieve an equal game. There are a variety of pawn moves, including central plans with ...e6, ...c5, ...d5, or the capture at e5. Flank options include ...g6 and ...g5. A final plan is moving the queen to d5, though that doesn't make a whole lot of sense.

CZECH DEFENSE - OPTIONS AT MOVE 7

1.e4 d6; 2.d4 Nf6; 3.Nc3 c6; 4.f4 Qa5; 5.e5 Ne4; 6.Bd3 Nxc3; 7.Qd2
Option 1: 7...e6
Option 2: 7...d5
Option 3: 7...g6
Option 4: 7...g5
Option 5: 7...Qd5
Option 6: 7...c5
Option 7: 7...dxe5

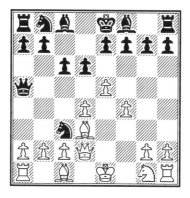

CZECH DEFENSE, MOVE 7
Option 1: 7...e6

This locks in the bishop at c8.

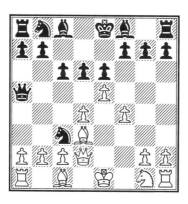

8.bxc3 c5 (8...d5; 9.Nf3 c5; 10.c4 Qxd2+; 11.Bxd2 dxc4; 12.Bxc4 cxd4; 13.Nxd4 transposes to a later point in the game.) 9.Ne2 d5; 10.c4 Qxd2+; 11.Bxd2 dxc4; 12.Bxc4 cxd4; 13.Nxd4 gives White a strong endgame.

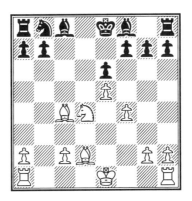

Black is way behind in development and space, Katalimov – Ufimtsev, Kazakhstan 1968.

CZECH DEFENSE, MOVE 7
Option 2: 7...d5
This move is solid, but inflexible.

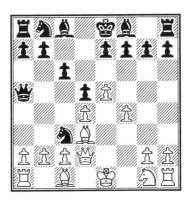

8.bxc3. 8...g6 (8...e6; 9.Nf3 c5; 10.c4 Qxd2+; 11.Bxd2 dxc4; 12.Bxc4 cxd4; 13.Nxd4 once again reaches the Katalimov – Ufimtsev endgame mentioned above in Option 1.) 9.Nf3 Bh6; (9...e6; 10.0-0 b6; 11.a4 Ba6; 12.Qe2 Bxd3; 13.cxd3 Qa6 was agreed drawn in Kulaots – Fridman, World Junior Championship 1996. Still, White has every reason to play on, as Black is still far from equality.) 10.0-0 Bf5; 11.Bxf5 gxf5; 12.e6 f6; 13.Nh4 Bf8; 14.Rb1 Qc7; 15.Qe2 h5; 16.Nxf5 Na6; 17.Rf3 0-0-0; 18.c4 and White has a clear advantage on the queenside and in the center, Pelikian – Blank, Sao Paulo 1996.

CZECH DEFENSE, MOVE 7
Option 3: 7...g6
This has no real independent significance.

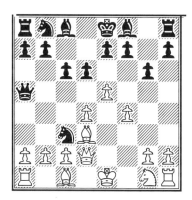

8.bxc3 dxe5 (8...Bf5; 9.Nf3 Nd7; 10.0-0 e6 is Stefanovski – Redzepagic, Struga 1991, and here 11.Rb1 is the most promising move.) 9.fxe5 transposes to the 7...dxe5 line.

CZECH DEFENSE, MOVE 7
Option 4: 7...g5
Such a radical move is hardly justified by Black's lagging development.

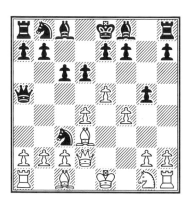

Now 8.Qxc3 Qxc3+; 9.bxc3 gxf4; 10.Bxf4 gave White a better game in Hennings – Hausner, Prague 1986.

CZECH DEFENSE, MOVE 7
Option 5: 7...Qd5

The queen seems to have a lot of scope here, but it cannot stay on the square forever.

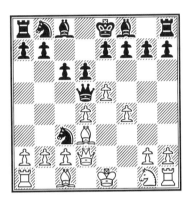

8.bxc3 c5; 9.Nf3 c4; 10.Be2 Bf5; 11.0-0 e6; 12.Ng5 h6; 13.g4 hxg5; 14.gxf5 exf5; 15.Bf3 Qb5; 16.Qg2 Nc6; 17.Qxg5 was a bit better for White in Theis – Palsson, Postal 1995.

CZECH DEFENSE, MOVE 7
Option 6: 7...c5!?

This is an interesting attempt to undermine the center.

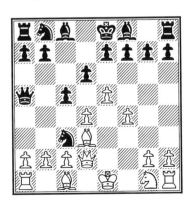

8.bxc3 d5; 9.Nf3 (9.c4 Qxd2+; 10.Bxd2 dxc4; 11.Bxc4 cxd4; 12.Nf3 Nc6 is not as good as the Katalimov – Ufimtsev endgame, because White has not regained the pawn at d4. Nevertheless, there is sufficient compensation in the advanced development, and I think that White can even afford 13.Rb1 e6; 14.Ke2 with the idea of bringing the king to d3 and grabbing the pawn. Black's bishop at c8 remains ineffective.) 9...Bg4 10.Rb1 Bxf3; 11.gxf3 c4; 12.Bf1 Qxa2; 13.Rxb7 Qa6; 14.Rb1 g6; 15.f5 gxf5; 16.Rg1 Nd7; 17.Be2 e6; 18.Qg5 Qa2; 19.Rb7 with a very complicated position in Timman – Hodgson, Biel 1995.

CZECH DEFENSE, MOVE 7
Option 7: 7...dxe5
This is the most interesting line. Two files are opened, one for use by each side.

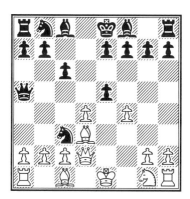

8.fxe5 g6. 8...c5; 9.Qxc3 Qxc3+; 10.bxc3 Nc6; 11.Be3 was played in Pieri – Valguarnera, Porto San Giorgio 1994. White has a better game because of advanced development and greater control of the center. **9.bxc3 Bh6.** Here we have another trap, though Black may have nothing better.
   10.Qxh6! Qxc3+; 11.Ke2 Qxa1. 11...Bg4+; 12.Nf3 Na6; 13.Be3 Nb4; 14.Bd2 Qxd4; 15.Bxb4 Qxb4; 16.Rab1 Qa5; 17.Rxb7 and Black is in deep trouble, Grabarczyk – Kiedrowicz, Polan Team Championship 1995. **12.Qg7 Rf8; 13.Nf3.** This presents the threat of Bh6. So Black extricates the queen with **13...Qxa2; 14.Bh6 Nd7; 15.Ng5!**

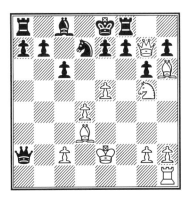

White continues to attack. Theory says the line is excellent for White, but I am critical of some of the analysis. White may have enough for the material, but were we not enamored of gambit play in general I might not be comfortable with the position.

15...Qd5. 15...b6; 16.e6! Ba6 (16...fxe6; 17.Nxh7 Nf6; 18.Qxf8+ Kd7; 19.Nxf6+ exf6; 20.Qf7+ wins for White.) 17.exd7+ Kxd7; 18.Bxa6 Qxa6+; 19.Kf2 Qc4; 20.Re1 and White's attack is worth the material. Black's rooks have no open files to use. 20...Rfe8; 21.Kg1 f6; 22.Ne6 Qb4; 23.Re2 Qb5; 24.Re1 Qa5; 25.Re3 Qb4.

Black's aimless play is indicative of the difficulties presented by the position. 26.h4 a5; 27.c3 Qb1+; 28.Kh2 Qf5; 29.Qf7 Qd5; 30.c4 Qh5; 31.Bf4 Qxh4+; 32.Kg1 g5. White now cleaned up quickly. 33.Nc5+ bxc5; 34.Qe6+ Kd8; 35.dxc5 Qxf4; 36.Rd3+ Kc7; 37.Qd7+ Black resigned as mate follows next move, Finkel – Oratovsky, Israel 1994.

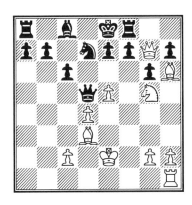

Now the theory goes **16.Rf1 Qxg2+; 17.Ke1 Qxh2; 18.Rxf7 Qh4+; 19.Kd2.** This is given as clearly better for White by Finkel, but I am not at all convinced. **19...Qxg5+!; 20.Bxg5 Rxf7.** Black has two rooks and three pawns for the queen. **21.Qg8+ Nf8; 22.d5** looks like the best White has since the pawn cannot be captured because of Bb5+. After **22...Bg4; 23.e6 Rf3; 24.Qg7.** The threat at e7 may be good enough. **24...0–0–0; 25.Qxe7 Rxd5; 26.Qe8+ Kc7; 27.Qe7+** and fortunately Black cannot escape to b6 because of Qb4+, winning the bishop at g4. **27...Kc8; 28.Qe8+** then draws.

But I don't think we need to abandon the idea of winning in the main line. In the position of the diagram I have found a new resource for White. 16.e6 is worth testing. 16...Qxg2+ is met by 17.Ke3 and the assault on f7 forces the advance of the f-pawn, for example, 17...f5 which does, at least, threaten checkmate at f4! After 18.exd7+ Kxd7; 19.Qxf8 Qxh1; 20.Nf3 and White will bring the knight to e5 with check.

At the very least there is the threat of Ne5+, Qxe7+ and checks along the a3-f8 diagonal to reach a draw. The bishop at h6 can come in to deliver lethal blows in many circumstances.

ALEKHINE DEFENSE
· KREJCIK VARIATION ·

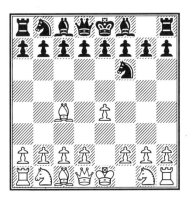

OPENING MOVES

1. e4　Nf6
2. Bc4

OVERVIEW

The **Krejcik Variation** is the only reasonable gambit try against the Alekhine Defense, but it does not have a good reputation. White does not have a positional basis for giving up an important central pawn. Here though, White sacrifices a pawn for a little action.

The idea is to capture at f7, then use a check at h5 to bring the queen to a position where it can, sooner or later, recover the piece by capturing the enemy knight. This is a time-consuming procedure, but most of it can be accomplished with a series of checks, preserving the initiative. After a few forced moves, we wind up with a rather strange position where neither side can boast of any significant development.

The opening is a gambit in the sense that material is sacrificed, but it will even out quickly.

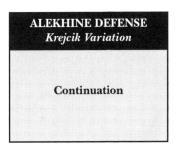

ALEKHINE DEFENSE
Krejcik Variation

Continuation

Black should capture the pawn, of course.

2...Nxe4. 2...e5 would transpose to the Bishop's Game, but then you can always play the gambit variation with 3.d4!?

2...b5 is the Laaber Gambit. Black offers the pawn to lure the bishop off the critical diagonal. 3.Bb3 is the correct reply. After 3...Bb7 (3...Nxe4; 4.Bxf7+ Kxf7; 5.Qh5+ is even better for White than in our main line.) 4.d3 The game is no longer a gambit. Black can try the aggressive 4...c5, but after 5.Nc3, the pawn is a target.

3.Bxf7+. If you don't play this move, there is nothing at all to show for the material. **3...Kxf7; 4.Qh5+.**

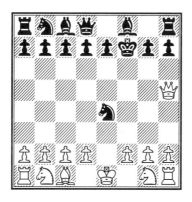

4...Kg8. 4...g6; 5.Qd5+ e6; 6.Qxe4 Bg7 is the other form of defense, for example 7.Nf3 Rf8; 8.d4 d5; 9.Qd3 Nc6; 10.Bg5 Qd6; 11.Nc3 a6; 12.0-0-0 Kg8; 13.h4 (13.Rhe1 is more promising, and should be advantageous for White, who should be working on the weakness at e6 and keep control of e5.) 13...Rxf3!?; 14.Qxf3 Nxd4; 15.Qg3 Qxg3; 16.fxg3 h6; 17.Bd8 c6; 18.Bb6 e5; 19.Bxd4 exd4; 20.Ne2 and White was better in Winge – Kaiser, Eikamp 1982.

5.Qd5+ e6; 6.Qxe4 d5; 7.Qe2 c5.

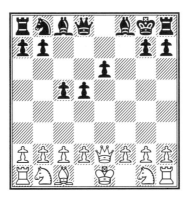

The position was reached in a correspondence game, Schober – Packroff, Postal. Black will develop rapidly with good attacking chances. The Black king is relatively safe at g8, and the inability to develop the rook from h8 is only a minor problem.

8.Nf3 Nc6; 9.0–0. 9.d3 Bd6; 10.Nc3 h6; 11.Bd2 Kh7; 12.d4 cxd4; 13.Nxd4 Nxd4; 14.Qd3+ Nf5; 15.g4 Rf8; 16.0-0-0 Qf6; 17.h4 Qd4 was clearly better for Black in Jongman – Van der Klashorst, Netherlands Postal Championship 1986.

9...Bd7; 10.c3 Bd6; 11.d4 Qf6; 12.Bg5 Qg6; 13.Bh4 Re8; 14.Nbd2 h6.

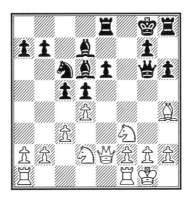

Black will continue with ...Kh7 and ...Rhf8, but the chances remain about even. White can chip away at the pawns in the center and try to make the best possible use of the open lines.

SCANDINAVIAN DEFENSE
• Tennison Gambit •

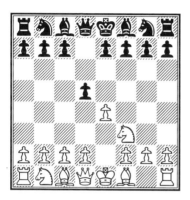

OPENING MOVES
1.Nf3   d5
2.e4

OVERVIEW

The **Tennison Gambit** is a radical attempt to alter the opening landscape with a gambit which encourages Black to create weaknesses early in the game. It is not sound, and most sensible defensive plans will suffice to get out of the opening alive as Black.

Still, if you want to play a gambit in every game as White, you will need to be reckless on occasion! So don't worry that Black can defend against your immediate threats. You can play this gambit in the style of Charousek, and patiently wait for your pressure to build to a point where your opponent must make a material or positional concession to maintain the pressure.

In a tournament situation your opponent is likely to crack and make that one small error that gives you the chance to close in for the kill or make a transition to a favorable endgame. Thus, when playing the Tennison, be patient, wait for mistake, and then close in for the finish!

SCANDINAVIAN DEFENSE	
Tennison Gambit	
2...dxe4; 3.Ng5	
Options at move 3	172
Option 1: 3...e5	172
Option 2: 3...f5!?	173
Option 3: 3...Qd5	174
Option 4: 3...Bf5	177
Option 5: 3...Nf6	177

2...dxe4; 3.Ng5.

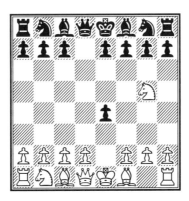

There are several tries, all involving central squares. The e-pawn can go to e5 to enable development of the bishop from f8. The pawn at e4 can also be defended by the weakening move 3...f5, or with a bishop at f5, or even with the queen! The most reasonable move, however, which we will save for last, is the simple defensive and developing move 3...Nf6.

TENNISON GAMBIT - OPTIONS AT MOVE 3
1.Nf3 d5; 2.e4 dxe4; 3.Ng5
Option 1: 3...e5
Option 2: 3...f5
Option 3: 3...Qd5
Option 4: 3...Bf5
Option 5: 3...Nf6

TENNISON GAMBIT, MOVE 3
Option 1: 3...e5

This is a principled move. Black opens lines for the bishop and queen, and attacks the knight at g5. There is really no downside. The weakness of f7 is normal in a King Pawn Game. This is my preferred reply.

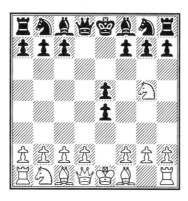

4.Nxe4 f5 is a position I recommend for Black in the companion book, *Gambit Opening Repertoire for Black*. But that is not to say the White side is unplayable. Indeed, after 5.Ng3 Nf6; 6.Bc4 Nc6; 7.0-0, Black will find it difficult to castle.

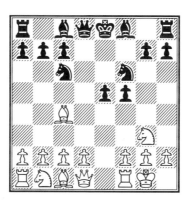

Nevertheless, I admit that I'd still prefer to be playing Black. It is hard to force a gambit in the Scandinavian, and if you want to enjoy the other exciting positions in this chapter, you have to be willing to put up with this.

TENNISON GAMBIT, MOVE 3
Option 2: 3...f5!?
This creates many weaknesses on the light squares, but is better than its reputation, so White must be careful.

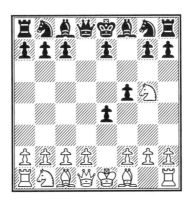

4.Bc4 Nh6 is the natural continuation.

A) 5.d3 exd3; 6.0-0! is the line gambit lovers will prefer. 6...dxc2 7.Qxc2 A1) 7...Nc6; 8.Rd1 Nd4; 9.Rxd4! Qxd4; 10.Be3 Qf6; 11.Nc3 c6; 12.Rd1 f4? (12...Bd7; 13.Qb3 0-0-0; 14.Ne6 gives White enough compensation for the pawns.) 13.Nb5! Qe5 (13...cxb5??; 14.Bxb5+ and mate in 3.) 14.Qe4! and Black lost in Lutes – Felt, Indianapolis (blitz) 1969.

A2) 7...e5; 8.Rd1 Bd6; (8...Qf6 is stronger. 9.Nc3 c6; 10.Qb3 provides compensation for at least one of the pawns.)

B) 5.Nxh7?! is not as good as it looks: 5...Rxh7 (5...g6!, suggested by Moser, keeps the game level.) 6.Qh5+ Kd7; 7.Qg6 Rh8; 8.Be6+ Kc6; 9.Bxc8+ Qd6; 10.Qe8+ Kb6; 11.Qa4. Black resigned in Tennison – Anonymous, New Orleans 1891. Tennison gives the possible conclusion: 11...Qc6; 12.Qb3+ Ka6; 13.Nc3, answering any move with Bxb7+, Qa4+ and Qb5#

TENNISON GAMBIT, MOVE 3
Option 3: 3...Qd5
Black can stubbornly hang on to the pawn.

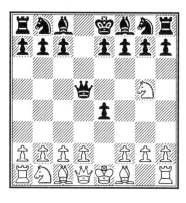

A) 4.d3 exd3; 5.Nc3 Qe5+; 6.Be3 dxc2; 7.Qd5

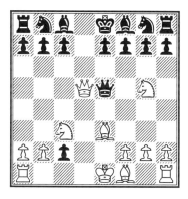

What an amazing sight! White has sacrificed three pawns and now offers an exchange of queens. But Black cannot accept! 7...Qf6 (7...Qxd5; 8.Nxd5 h6; 9.Nxc7+ Kd8; 10.Nxa8 hxg5; 11.Bxa7 Nc6; 12.Bb6+ Kd7; 13.Rc1 and White has an extra exchange.) 8.Bd3. This is analysis by Jakobetz, Somlai and Varnusz.

I can't quite agree with their evaluation of a clear advantage for White, but do think that White has enough compensation, after, say, 8...c6; 9.Qb3 h6; 10.Nce4 Qg6; 11.Nc5 (11.Nd6+ Qxd6; 12.Nxf7 Qxd3; 13.Qxd3 Kxf7; 14.Qxc2 does not appeal to me.) 11...Qf6; 12.Nh7 (12.Nce4 Qg6; 13.Nc5 Qf6 bails to a draw.) 12...Qe5; 13.Nxf8 Kxf8; 14.Bxc2 Nf6; 15.Rd1 Nbd7; 16.Nxd7+ Nxd7; 17.0-0 and White is fully developed, while Black has little prospect of getting the rooks into the game and the king may never be safe.

Worth two pawns? I am not sure, but if you are going to play gambits, you ought to be able to appreciate your compensation here.

B) 4.h4 can be considered as a safer, if less interesting, alternative. 4...Nf6; 5.Nc3 Qe5.

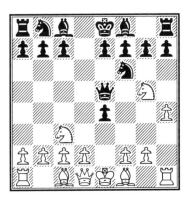

6.Bc4 e6; 7.Qe2 Nc6 is roughly level, according to Benjamin, whose analysis has received a practical test: 8.Bb5 (8.Ngxe4 Nxe4; 9.Nxe4 Nd4 leads to undesirable consequences for White.) 8...Bd7; 9.Ngxe4 Nxe4; 10.Qxe4 Qxe4+; 11.Nxe4 a6.

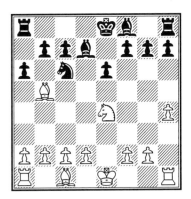

12.Ba4 (12.Bxc6 Bxc6; 13.d3 is likely to be drawn in the end, as ...f5 is not such a great threat. Still, Black is better.) 12...b5; 13.Bb3 Nd4; 14.c3 (14.d3 Nxb3; 15.axb3 would maintain the balance.) 14...Nxb3; 15.axb3 left Black with the bishop pair and better pawns, which adds up to the much better game in Bullockus – Wegener, World Senior Championship 1996.

TENNISON GAMBIT, MOVE 3
Option 4: 3...Bf5

The bishop can be driven back with tempo, and then the White bishop can be aimed at the weakling on e4.

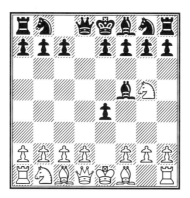

4.g4 Bg6; 5.Bg2 Nf6; 6.Nc3 Nc6; 7.Ngxe4 e6; 8.Nxf6+ Qxf6; 9.d3 Bd6; 10.Bxc6+ bxc6; 11.Be3 Ke7; 12.h4 h6; 13.Qe2 provided a lively game in Bendic – Melchor, Postal 1992.

TENNISON GAMBIT, MOVE 3
Option 5: 3...Nf6.

The development of the knight, protecting the pawn, is the most obvious move for Black.

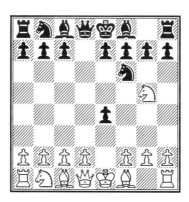

4.Bc4 e6; 5.Qe2!?. More common is Nc3, but this move is at least as good. **5...h6.** 5...Nc6; 6.Nxe4 Nd4; 7.Nxf6+ Qxf6; 8.Qe4 and White will play c3 and d4 with a strong position. **6.Nxe4 Nxe4; 7.Qxe4.**

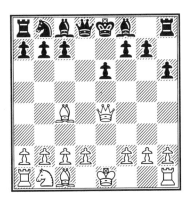

White has two pieces developed and the queen sits safely in the middle of the board. Black will have problems developing the bishop from c8. So White's position is already comfortable.

7...Nd7; 8.d3 Nf6; 9.Qf3 Bd6; 10.Nc3 0-0.

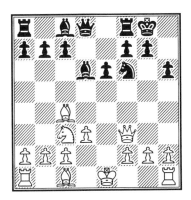

11.g4! The reason that White does not castle is that the kingside attack will take the form of a pawnstorm. Therefore, the king is safer on the other side of the board. **11...Nh7; 12.h4 Qf6.** Black attempts to get the queens off the board. White will not cooperate. **13.Qe2 Bb4; 14.Bd2 b5.**

This was Black's desperate reaction in Vazquez – Corzo, Havana 1900. In the famous 8th edition of the *Bilguer Handbuch*, Schlechter and Berger recommend 15.g5! instead of capturing the pawn at b5. The attack on the kingside should prove successful.

OWEN DEFENSE

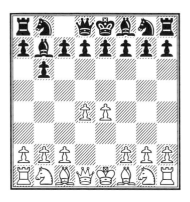

OPENING MOVES
1.e4   b6
2.d4   Bb7

The **Owen Defense** is disreputable and White can get an advantage with straightforward development. There is no need for a gambit here. None at all. But when a true gambiteer wants to explore the possibilities, there are some to be found. Black's slow defense hardly prevents you from striving for massive complications against this second rate defense.

Of course, classical players will simply develop knights at c3 and f3, a bishop at c4, and aim for rapid castling. That's objectively the best way to play. It is hardly likely to appeal, however, to a gambiteer!

I've chosen some very sharp lines for your consideration. The variations presented below are easier to play as White. Black must calculate precisely. There is even one variation where we go three pawns down and then offer to exchange queens, which will come as quite a shock to the unprepared (or under-prepared) opponent.

People who play the Owen count on a certain element of surprise, but we can show them that Black does not have a monopoly on that commodity!

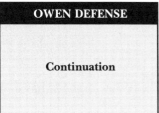

OWEN DEFENSE

Continuation

3.Bd3 f5?! 3...Nf6 is the normal move. Then 4.Qe2 Nc6; 5.c3 e5; 6.Nf3 exd4; 7.e5 Nd5; 8.Be4 is a spirited gambit continuation, Schendstok – Wind, The Hague 1979.

3...e6 is often seen. 4.Qe2 Be7; 5.f4 c5; 6.c3 Nf6; 7.Nf3 0-0 is Boden – Owen, London 1858, and here I think that 8.e5 is good for White.

4.exf5 Bxg2; 5.Qh5+ g6; 6.fxg6.

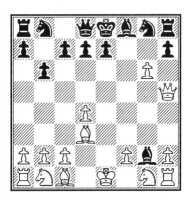

This wild line is typical of openings where White plays e4 and Black fianchettoes on the queenside. The f-pawn is sacrificed to get the e-pawn out of the way, with a capture at g2 trapping the rook. But in the meantime, Black's kingside gets shredded.

6...Bg7. The blunder 6...Nf6??; 7.gxh7+ Nxh5; 8.Bg6# dates back to Greco in the 17th century! **7.gxh7+ Kf8.**

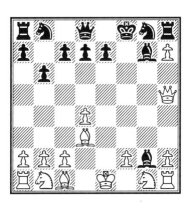

White actually has a pleasant choice between three lines here. **8.Nf3.**

8.hxg8+ and 8.Ne2. 8... Kxg8 (Not 8...Rxg8??; 9.Nf3 Bxh1; 10.Ng5 Qe8; 11.Nh7# Standler – Mukhin, Postal 1973.) 9.Qg4 Bxh1.

This position has been studied deeply and Black has generally been doing well, but the last word has not been spoken. 10.h4 Bd5! 11.h5 Be6 (11...Kf8; 12.Nc3 Bf7; 13.Bg6 Nc6; 14.Bxf7 Kxf7; 15.Qg6+ Kf8; 16.h6 Bxd4; 17.h7 Bg7; 18.Bh6 Bxh6; 19.Qxh6+ Kf7; 20.Nf3 and the Black king is about to topple, Navarro – Espinosa, Postal 1986.) 12.Qg2 Rxh5!; 13.Qxa8 Bd5; 14.Qxa7 Nc6; 15.Qa4 Rh1; 16.Kf1 Nxd4; 17.Nd2! is the trick that White overlooked.(17.Bc4 Bxc4+; 18.Qxc4+ d5 is Schmit – Vitolins, Latvia 1969, and here White could play 19.Qd3 with a good game.)

8.Ne2 is considered best by Wall, who points out the danger if Black takes the rook. 8...Bxh1; 9.Nf4 Nf6; 10.Ng6+ Ke8; 11.Nxh8+ Nxh5; 12.Bg6+ Kf8; 13.Bxh5 e5; 14.Ng6+ Kf7; 15.Nxe5+ Ke6; 16.Bg4+ Kd5; 17.Bf4 Ke4 (17...Kxd4! is an improvement. White has only a piece and a couple of pawns for the queen. Still, all is not lost. 18.Nc3 Kc5; 19.0-0-0 forces Black to return at least another piece to avoid mate.) 18.Be3 with the threat of Nc3 mate.

Returning to the Main Line
8...Nf6; 9.Qg6 Bxf3!; 10.Rg1 Rxh7; 11.Qg3 Be4.

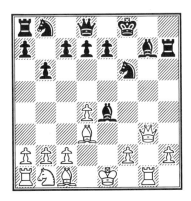

12.Bxe4 Nxe4; 13.Qf3+ Kg8. 13...Nf6; 14.Qxa8 Rxh2 (14...d5 15.Nc3 c6; 16.Bf4 Nfd7; 17.0-0-0 e5; 18.dxe5 Qc7; 19.Rxg7 Kxg7; 20.Nxd5 cxd5; 21.Qxd5 Nf8; 22.Rg1+ Black resigned, Kolenbrander – Perrenet, Postal 1979.) 15.Bf4 Rh4; 16.Qg2 Rg4; 17.Bg3 and White is better, Dallmann – Ewald, Leipzig 1996.
14.Qxe4 d5; 15.Qe6+ Kh8; 16.Nc3 with a much better game for White in Carlsson – Frausing, Denmark 1977.

LAST THOUGHTS

In the preceding chapters you have been provided with a powerful arsenal of gambit weapons to use in your games. I hope you find not only success, but also some creative combinations and attacks. As a gambiteer, you have chosen to play the opening boldly, relentlessly pursuing the enemy king.

You'll win some games, lose some games, and draw a few, too. When you win, make sure you try to find the point in the game where your opponent made the critical error, and figure out what you would have done against a better defense. After a loss, find your own errors, especially the first one. Study that position and see if you can find an improvement.

Computer programs can be a big help here! Use them to identify tactical blunders. Learn from your mistakes and try not to repeat them. If the game was drawn, look for improvements for either side. Surely someone missed a stronger move along the way. In any case, you need to feel confident in your repertoire whenever you sit down to play. You should be satisfied with the results of the opening in each game. Otherwise you need to re-examine the opening and look for a different approach, if necessary.

Don't get discouraged if you fail to spot tactical opportunities at first. Your recognition of important patterns will increase greatly as you gain more experience with the openings. Even if you forget the proper moves, aim for the kinds of attacks you have seen in the illustrative games. When you run out of theory, improvise! Relax, target the enemy king, keep in mind transitions to favorable endgames, and let loose on the opponent with all the fury you can muster!

SUGGESTIONS FOR FURTHER READING

Göring Gambit
 How to Play the Göring Gambit by Eric Schiller, Chess Enterprises
 Winning with the Göring Gambit by Ken Smith/John Hall, Chess Digest

Alapin Gambit,
 Alapin French by Tim Sawyer, Thinker's Press

Halasz Gambit, Ulysses Gambit
 Gambit-Revue (4 issues per year, in German), Schachverlag Manfred
 Maedler, Lilienthal Str. 52, 4000 Dusseldorf 30, Germany

Smith-Morra Gambit
 Winning with the Smith Morra Gambit by Graham Burgess, Batsford.

Pirc and Modern Defense
 The Complete Pirc by John Nunn, B.T. Batsford

Tennison Gambit
 Tennison Gambit by W. John Lutes, Chess Enterprises

Owen Defense
 Owen's Defense by Bill Wall, Chess Enterprises

Gambits (General)
 Gambit-Revue (as above)
 The Complete Book of Gambits by Raymond Keene, B.T. Batsford

Unorthodox Openings
 Unorthodox Chess Openings by Eric Schiller, Cardoza Publishing

CARDOZA PUBLISHING CHESS BOOKS

STANDARD CHESS OPENINGS by *Eric Schiller* - The new definitive standard on opening chess play in the 20th century, this comprehensive guide covers every important chess opening and variation ever played and currently in vogue. In all, more than 3,000 opening strategies are presented! Differing from previous opening books which rely almost exclusively on bare notation, *SCO* features substantial discussion and analysis on each opening so that you learn and understand the concepts behind them. Includes more than 250 completely annotated games (including a game representative of each major opening) and more than 1,000 diagrams! For modern players at any level, this is the standard reference book necessary for competitive play. *A must have for serious chess players!!!* 768 pages, $24.95

UNORTHODOX CHESS OPENINGS by *Eric Schiller* - The exciting guide to all the major unorthodox openings used by chess players, contains more than 1,500 weird, contentious, controversial, unconventional, arrogant, and outright strange opening strategies. From their tricky tactical surprises to their bizarre names, these openings fly in the face of tradition. You'll meet such openings as the Orangutang, Raptor Variation, Halloween Gambit, Double Duck, Frankenstein-Dracula Variation, and even the Drunken King! These openings are a sexy and exotic way to spice up a game and a great weapon to spring on unsuspecting and often unprepared opponents. More than 750 diagrams show essential positions. 528 pages, $24.95

WORLD CHAMPION OPENINGS by *Eric Schiller* - This serious reference work covers the essential opening theory and moves of every major chess opening and variation as played by *all* the world champions. Reading as much like an encyclopedia of the must-know openings crucial to every chess player's knowledge as a powerful tool showing the insights, concepts and secrets as used by the greatest players of all time, *World Champion Openings (WCO)* covers an astounding 100 crucial openings in full conceptual detail (with 100 actual games from the champions themselves)! *A must-have book for serious chess players.* 384 pages, $16.95

WORLD CHAMPION COMBINATIONS by *Keene and Schiller* - Learn the insights, concepts and moves of the greatest combinations ever by the greatest players who ever lived. From Morphy to Alekhine, to Fischer to Kasparov, the incredible combinations and brilliant sacrifices of the 13 World Champions are collected here in the most insightful combinations book written. Packed with fascinating strategems, 50 annotated games, and great practical advice for your own games, this is a great companion guide to *World Champion Openings*. 264 pages, $16.95.

BEGINNING CHESS PLAY by *Bill Robertie* - Step-by-step approach uses 113 diagrams to teach novices the basic principles of chess. Covers opening, middle and end game strategies, principles of development, pawn structure, checkmates, openings and defenses, how to write and read chess notation, join a chess club, play in tournaments, use a chess clock, and get rated. Two annotated games illlustrate strategic thinking for easy learning. 144 pages, $9.95

WINNING CHESS OPENINGS by *Bill Robertie* - Shows concepts and best opening moves of more than 25 essential openings from Black's and White's perspectives: King's Gambit, Center Game, Scotch Game, Giucco Piano, Vienna Game, Bishop's Opening, Ruy Lopez, French, Caro-Kann, Sicilian, Alekhine, Pirc, Modern, Queen's Gambit, Nimzo-Indian, Queen's Indian, Dutch, King's Indian, Benoni, English, Bird's, Reti's, and King's Indian Attack. Examples from 25 grandmasters and champions including Fischer and Kasparov. 144 pages, $9.95

MASTER CHECKMATE STRATEGY by *Bill Robertie* - Learn all the basic combinations, plus advanced, surprising and unconventional mates, and the most effective pieces needed to win. Players learn how to mate opponents with just a pawn advantage; how to work two rooks into an unstoppable attack; how to wield a queen advantage with deadly intent; how to coordinate movements by pieces of differing strengths into indefensible positions of their opponents; when it's best to have a knight, and when a bishop to win. 144 pages, $9.95

WINNING CHESS TACTICS by *Bill Robertie* - 14 chapters of winning tactical concepts show the complete explanations and thinking behind every tactical concept: pins, single and double forks, double attacks, skewers, discovered and double checks, multiple threats - and other crushing tactics to gain an immediate edge over opponents. Learn the power tools of tactical play to become a stronger player. Includes guide to chess notation. 128 pages, $9.95

CARDOZA PUBLISHING CHESS BOOKS

THE BASICS OF WINNING CHESS by Jacob Cantrell - A great first book of chess, in one easy reading, beginner's learn the moves of the pieces, the basic rules and principles of play, the standard openings, and both Algebraic and English chess notation. The basic ideas of the winning concepts and strategies of middle and end game play are shown as well. Includes example games of great champions. 64 pages, $4.95.

GAMBIT OPENING REPERTOIRE FOR WHITE by Eric Schiller - Chessplayers who enjoy attacking from the very first move are rewarded here with a powerful repertoire of brilliant gambits. Starting off with 1.e4 or 1.d4 and then using such sharp weapons such as the Göring Gambit (Accepted and Declined), Halasz Gambit, Alapin Gambit, Ulysses Gambit, Short Attack and many more, to put great pressure on opponents, Schiller presents a complete attacking repertoire to use against the most popular defenses, including the Sicilian, French, Scandinavian, Caro-Kann, Pirc, Alekhine, and a host of Open Game situations. 192 pages, $14.95.

GAMBIT OPENING REPERTOIRE FOR BLACK by Eric Schiller - For players that like exciting no-holds-barred chess, this versatile gambit repertoire shows Black how to take charge with aggressive attacking defenses against any orthodox first White opening move; 1.e4, 1.d4 and 1.c4. Learn the Scandinavian Gambit against 1.e4, the Schara Gambit and Queen's Gambit Declined variations against 1.d4, and some flank and unorthodox gambits also. Black learns the secrets of seizing the initiative from White's hands, usually by investing a pawn or two, to begin powerful attacks that can send White to early defeat. 176 pages, $14.95.

BASIC ENDGAME STRATEGY, Kings, Pawns and Minor Pieces by Bill Robertie - Learn the basic checkmating principles and combinations needed to finish off opponents and claim victory at the chessboard. From the four basic checkmates using the King with the queen, rook, two bishops, and bishop/knight combination, to the basic King/pawn, King/Knight and King/Bishop endgames, chessplayers learn the essentials of translating small edges in the middlegame into decisive endgame victories. Learn the 50-move rule, and the combinations of pieces that can't force a checkmate against a lone King. 144 pages, $12.95.

301 TRICKY CHECKMATES by Fred Wilson and Bruce Alberston - Both a fascinating challenge and great training tool, this collection of two and three move checkmates is great for advanced beginning, intermediate and expert players. Mates are in order of difficulty, from the simple to very complex positions. Learn the standard patterns and stratagems for cornering the king: corridor and support mates, attraction and deflection sacrifices, pins and annihilation, the quiet move, and the dreaded *zugzwang*. Examples, drawn from actual games, illustrate a wide range of chess tactics from old classics right up to the 1990's. 192 pages, $9.95.

COMPLETE DEFENSE TO KING PAWN OPENINGS by Eric Schiller - Learn a complete defensive system against 1.e4. This powerful repertoire not only limits White's ability to obtain any significant opening advantage but allows Black to adopt the flexible Caro-Kann formation, the favorite weapon of many of the greatest chess players. All White's options are explained in detail, and a plan is given for Black to combat them all. Analysis is up-to-date and backed by examples drawn from games of top stars. Detailed index lets you follow the opening from the point of a specific player, or through its history. 240 pages, $16.95.

COMPLETE DEFENSE TO QUEEN PAWN OPENINGS by Eric Schiller - This aggressive counterattacking repertoire covers Black opening systems against virtually every chess opening except for 1.e4 (including most flank games), based on the exciting and powerful Tarrasch Defense, an opening that helped bring Championship titles to Kasparov and Spassky. Black learns to effectively use the Classical Tarrasch, Symmetrical Tarrasch, Asymmetrical Tarrasch, Marshall and Tarrasch Gambits, and Tarrasch without Nc3, to achieve an early equality or even an outright advantage in the first few moves. 240 pages, $16.95.

SECRETS OF THE SICILIAN DRAGON by GM Eduard Gufeld and Eric Schiller - The mighty Dragon Variation of the Sicilian Defense is one of the most exciting openings in chess. Everything from opening piece formation to the endgame, including clear explanations of all the key strategic and tactical ideas, is covered in full conceptual detail. Instead of memorizing a jungle of variations, you learn the really important ideas behind the opening, and how to adapt them at the chessboard. Special sections on the heroes of the Dragon show how the greatest players handle the opening. The most instructive book on the Dragon ever written! 160 pages, $14.95.

CARDOZA PUBLISHING CHESS BOOKS

ENCYCLOPEDIA OF CHESS WISDOM, The Essential Concepts and Strategies of Smart Chess Play by Eric Schiller - The most important concepts, strategies, tactics, wisdom, and thinking that every chessplayer must know, plus the gold nuggets of knowledge behind every attack and defense, is collected together in one highly focused volume. From opening, middle and endgame strategy, to psychological warfare and tournament tactics, the *Encyclopedia of Chess Wisdom* forms the blueprint of power play and advantage at the chess board. Step-by-step, the reader is taken through the thinking behind each essential concept, and through examples, discussions, and diagrams, shown the full impact on the game's direction. You even learn how to correctly study chess to become a chess master. 400 pages, $19.95.

BASIC ENDGAME STRATEGY: Rooks and Queens by Bill Robertie - The companion guide to *Basic Endgame Strategy: Kings, Pawns and Minor Pieces*, shows the basic checkmating principles and combinations needed to finish off opponents using the the Queen and Rook with King combinations.. You'll learn to translate middlegame advantages into decisive endgame victories, how to create passed pawns, use the King as a weapon, clear the way for rook mates, and recognize the combinations that appear in endgames. 144 pages, $12.95.

EXCELLENT CHESS BOOKS - OTHER PUBLISHERS
- OPENINGS -

HOW TO PLAY THE TORRE by Eric Schiller - One of Schiller's best-selling books, the 19 chapters on this fabulous and aggressive White opening (1. d4 Nf6; 2. Nf3 e6; 3. Bg5) will make opponents shudder and get you excited about chess all over again. Insightful analysis, completely annotated games get you ready to win! 210 pages, $17.50.

A BLACK DEFENSIVE SYSTEM WITH 1...D6 by Andrew Soltis - This Black reply - so rarely played that it doesn't even have a name - throws many opponents off their rote attack and can lead to a decisive positional advantage. Use this surprisingly strong system to give you the edge against unprepared opponents. 166 pages, $16.50.

BLACK TO PLAY CLASSICAL DEFENSES AND WIN by Eric Schiller - *Shows you how to develop a complete opening repertoire as black.* Emerge from *any* opening with a playable position, fighting for the center from the very first move. Defend against the Ruy Lopez, Italian Game, King's Gambit, King's Indian, many more. 166 pages, $16.50.

ROMANTIC KING'S GAMBIT IN GAMES & ANALYSIS by Santasiere & Smith - The most comprehensive collection of theory and games (137) on this adventurous opening is filled with annotations and "color" on the greatest King's Gambits played and the players. Makes you *want* to play! Very readable; packed with great concepts. 233 pages, $17.50.

WHITE TO PLAY 1.E4 AND WIN by Eric Schiller - *Shows you how to develop a complete opening system as white beginning 1. e4.* Learn the recommended opening lines to all the major systems as white, and how to handle any defense black throws back. Covers the Sicilian, French, Caro-Kann, Scandinavia; many more. 166 pages, $16.50.

HOW TO PLAY THE SICILIAN DEFENSE AGAINST ALL WHITE POSSIBILITIES by Andrew Soltis - Terrific book emphasizes understanding the ideas behind the Sicilian so that you'll not only play well against any sound White opening - you'll actually look forward to 1.e4! Learn to turn the Sicilian into a fighting offensive line. 184 pages, $13.95.

BIG BOOK OF BUSTS by Schiller & Watson - Learn how to defend against 70 dangerous and annoying openings which are popular in amateur chess and can lead to defeat if unprepared, but can be refuted when you know how to take opponents off their favorite lines. Greet opponents with your own surprises! Recommended. 293 pages, $22.95.

- ENDGAMES -

ESSENTIAL CHESS ENDINGS EXPLAINED VOL. 1 by Jeremy Silman - This essential and enjoyable reference tool to mates and stalemates belongs in every chess player's library. Commentary on every move plus quizzes and many diagrams insure complete understanding. All basic positions covered, plus many advanced ones. 221 pages, $16.50.

ESSENTIAL CHESS ENDINGS EXPLAINED VOL. 2 *by Ken Smith* - This book assumes you know the basics of the 1st volume and takes you all the way to Master levels. Work through moves of 275 positions and learn as you go. There are explanations of every White and Black move so you know what's happening from both sides. 298 pages, $17.50.

- MIDDLEGAME/TACTICS/WINNING CONCEPTS -

CHESS TACTICS FOR ADVANCED PLAYERS *by Yuri Averbakh* - A great tactical book; complex combinations are brilliantly simpified to basic, easy-to-understand concepts you can use to win at chess. Learn the underlying structure of piece harmony and fortify skills through numerous exercises. Very instructive, a must read. 328 pages, $17.50.

BIG BOOK OF COMBINATIONS *by Eric Schiller* - Test your tactical ability in 1,000 brilliant combinations from actual games spanning the history of chess. Includes various degrees of difficulty from the easiest to the most difficult combinations. Unlike other combination books, this one provides no hints, so you'll have to work! 266 pages, $17.95.

STRATEGY FOR ADVANCED PLAYERS *by Eric Schiller* - Recommended for intermediate to advanced players, 45 insightful and very informative lessons illustrate the strategic and positional factors you need to know in middle and endgame play. Recommended highly as a tool to learn strategic chess and become a better player. 135 pages, $14.50.

HOW TO BECOME A CANDIDATE MASTER *by Alex Dunne* -The book that makes you *think* is packed with tips and inspiration; from a wide variety of openings in 50 fully annotated games to in-depth middle and end game discussions, the goal is to take your game up to the Expert level. A perennial favorite. 252 pages, $18.95.

KASPAROV EXPRESS™

SAITEK - The World Leader in Intelligent Electronic Games

VERSATILE AND FUN - An amazing 384 level/setting combinations includes fun levels for novices and challenging levels for experienced players. Economic powerful, and pocket size (approximately 5" x 61/2" x 1') this game is an unbeatable easy traveling companion.
GREAT INEXPENSIVE TRAVEL COMPANION! - Features different playing styles and strengths, 5 special coach modes, and teaching levels! Sensory-style chess board, peg type pieces, folding lid, LCD screen, take back and hint features, built-in chess clock that keeps track of time for both sides, and self-rating system. Memory holds an unfinished game for up to two years, gives you the complete package in an economical, handy travel-ready unit.
To order, send just $49.95 for the <u>Express</u>.

KASPAROV TRAVEL CHAMPION 2100

SAITEK - The World Leader in Intelligent Electronic Games

THE WORLD'S MOST POWERFUL HAND-HELD CHESS COMPUTER ANYWHERE! - This **super program** and **integrated training system** has an **official USCF rating of 2334!** This **awesome program** can beat over 99% of all chess players, yet it's still great for the novice. LCD shows principal variation, evaluation, search depth, and search mode counts.
64 SKILL LEVELS - 64 levels of skill and handicapping give you tons of **options** and **versatility**: Play against beginning, intermediate or advanced opponents (includes tournament time controls), play Blitz or Tournament, choose Active, Passive, or Complete style, or Tournament Opening Book, select **Brute Force** algorithm or the advanced Selective Search. Match your skill to the correct level for most **challenging** chess. You want it - it's all here!
To order, send just $129.95 for the <u>Kasparov Travel Champion 2100</u>.

KASPAROV TALKING COACH™

SAITEK - The World Leader in Intelligent Electronic Games

AMAZING NEW TALKING TECHNOLOGY - Wow everyone with this incredible table top computer chess unit that not only informs and encourages you throughout the game but provides tremendous flexibility for both playing and coaching. Even more amazing, this **talking chess computer** retails for under $100!

POWERFUL AND VERSATILE - SETTINGS FOR EVERYONE - Play at any level you like - **384 level/setting combinations** and a built-in library of 134 opening moves allow a full range of options. Beginners can use the levels and features to learn, intermediate players to become stronger, and higher level players to take the challenge head on.

GREAT FOR LEARNING - Improve your chess or play for fun! The user-selectable **Talking Coach** includes learning, coach and warning modes (lets you know if a piece is in take), while the smart hint key suggests moves when you need help. If you change your mind and want to see how a game plays out differently, use the take-back feature; it allows take back up to 6 moves.

READY FOR ACTION - Sensory style chess board comes with built-in handy storage compartment for the pieces. Turn off current game at any time and continue play later - computer remembers position for up to two years.

To order, send just $99.95 for the <u>Kasparov Talking Coach</u>.

KASPAROV CHESS GK2100™

SAITEK - The World Leader in Intelligent Electronic Games

THE BEST VALUE MONEY CAN BUY! - The **fabulous** Kasparov GK2100 is the **most popular** chess computer we sell. Using a super high speed **RISC** computer chip and rated at a **2334** USCF rating, you'll have consistent challenges and excitement. Coaching features and fun levels makes it suitable for novices; masters and experts will want to choose higher levels.

GREAT DESIGN - Packaged in a sleek, handsome cabinet suitable for your living room. No need to find a partner to play - **take on the Champion**!

POWERFUL PROGRAM FEATURES - **64 levels of play** include sudden death, tournament, problem solving and beginner's. Shows intended move and position evaluation, take back up to 50 moves, and user selectable **book openings library**. Also choose from **Active, Passive, Tournament, complete book, no book**. Select the high speed **Selective Search** or play against the powerful **Brute Force.** program. Thinks in opponents time for best realism. Shutoff, shut on memory - remembers game for 1 year!

GREAT FOR BEGINNERS AND MASTERS ALIKE! - This **awesome program** can beat over 99% of all regular chess players, yet it is still suitable for beginners and intermediate players: Simply set the skill level to the appropriate strength for the best challenges. Matching your skill to the correct level of play ensures a **challenging** and **exciting** game.

EVEN MORE FEATURES - Opening library of 35,000 moves, **large LCD** shows full information and keeps track of playing time. Modern ergonomic design goes well in living room.

To order, send $199.95 for the <u>Kasparov Chess GK2100</u>

CHESSWORKS UNLIMITED

Chess Software, Books, Tournaments, E-mail Instruction and Information

THE ONE STOP SOURCE FOR SERIOUS CHESS PLAYERS

Chessworks Unlimited, owned and operated by Eric Schiller, is a central information center where you can shop for high-quality chess software at affordable prices or find out about international chess events, editorials, and chess in general. You can also find out more information on Dr. Schiller's books and be the first to know about upcoming titles when they're hot off the press, and you can even arrange for online or email instruction and analysis!

Chessworks Unlimited organizes chess tournaments in Hawaii and Northern California. Visit our web site to see the latest listings!

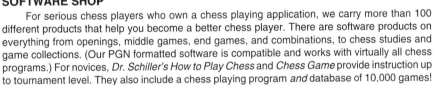

http://www.chessworks.com

THE CHESSWORKS UNLIMITED SOFTWARE SHOP

For serious chess players who own a chess playing application, we carry more than 100 different products that help you become a better chess player. There are software products on everything from openings, middle games, end games, and combinations, to chess studies and game collections. (Our PGN formatted software is compatible and works with virtually all chess programs.) For novices, *Dr. Schiller's How to Play Chess* and *Chess Game* provide instruction up to tournament level. They also include a chess playing program *and* database of 10,000 games!